Can I Control My Changing Emotions?

Answers to Questions Women Ask About Their Moods

Answers to Questions Women Ask

Can I Control My Changing Emotions?
Can I Afford Time for Friendships?
Can a Busy Christian Develop Her Spiritual Life?

Can I Control My Changing Emotions?

Answers to Questions Women Ask About Their Moods

Annie Chapman

Luci Shaw

Florence Littauer

BETHANY HOUSE PUBLISHERS
Minneapolis, Minnesota 55438

ANNIE CHAPMAN and her husband, singer-songwriter Steve, have ministered to families across the nation with their music and speaking. She is the author of three books with Bethany House Publishers, including *Smart Women Keep It Simple* and *Married Lovers, Married Friends*.

LUCI SHAW is past president of Harold Shaw Publishers and is known primarily as a poet and lecturer. Writer-in-residence at Regent College, Vancouver, her first book of prose, *God in the Dark*, met with critical acclaim and her workbook on journaling, *Life Path*, is the text for workshops that she leads across the continent.

FLORENCE LITTAUER is a well-known speaker and author of twenty books, including the national bestseller, *Personality Plus*. As founder and president of CLASS Speakers, Inc., her mission has been helping people understand themselves and communicate more effectively.

Contents

Part Three
My Private Battles

Epilogue

UNRAVELING THE MYSTERY CALLED EMOTIONS

ASK A WOMAN HOW she feels and the response may be, "It depends." Did the kids behave? Does her boss understand the pressure she's under? Was her husband's comment at breakfast encouraging? Do the extra five pounds she's carrying show?

The question "How do you feel?" is never a simple one because the answer is tied to so many variables. And, as women, the quality of our lives is largely determined by our emotional well-being. Though we may not want to admit it, our emotions often rule our attitudes and responses to others, ourselves, and God.

As Annie Chapman says, when it comes to getting a handle on our emotions, "age and experience make a difference." She remembers a time not long ago after giving a concert with her family when her emotions could have led her to make a less than pleasant comment to a fan. "I had changed into jeans and a sweatshirt and removed my makeup before heading out to a local restaurant. A woman who had attended the concert was at the restaurant and upon seeing me said, 'From a distance you look very young and pretty, but now that I see you up close, I see that you're not.' "

Annie's response was a polite "thank you," but she admits that just a few years ago she might not have been as gracious or in control of her emotions.

Ever since Eve wrestled with temptation, women have struggled with their emotions. We probably always will. Thankfully, though, the God who created us with such an intricate emotional makeup is also the God who dwells in us and prompts us to learn new ways to deal with our complex feelings and to appreciate our unique design.

In this book, Annie Chapman, Florence Littauer, and Luci Shaw—three prominent and respected Christians—address thirteen of the most common questions women ask about their emotions. As each candidly shares her own struggles of keeping her emotions in check, together they offer honest, from-the-heart insights that will enlighten and uplift you. And always, with compassion, the contributors provide wise and practical advice for coping with our ever-changing feelings.

The chapters in this book are based on conversations shared at a two-day forum held in Chicago in March 1991, as well as personal telephone interviews with each contributor. To supplement their insights, select chapters include excerpts from the pages of *Today's Christian Woman* magazine. Every chapter also features a section titled "Make It Happen," which offers practical ways you can quickly and easily implement the specific suggestions made in each chapter.

About the Contributors

Annie, Florence, and Luci are three diverse women— one laughs often and speaks with her hands, another is quiet and contemplative, and yet another, a mix of both. It is our hope that through the experiences of one of the contributors, or possibly a little of each, you'll see yourself and find the answers you need to understand fully your unique emotional makeup.

Annie Chapman lives just outside of Nashville and together with her husband, singer-songwriter Steve, they have ministered to families across the nation with their music and speaking. As the mother of two teenagers,

Nathan and Heidi, Annie knows all about juggling a thousand responsibilities while attempting to maintain a balanced emotional life. With a refreshing sense of humor and a delightfully direct manner, Annie's advice is both practical and proven. In addition to producing several albums, Annie and Steve have co-written *Married Lovers, Married Friends* (Bethany) and *Gifts Your Kids Can't Break* (Bethany). In her latest book, *Smart Women Keep It Simple* (Bethany), Annie offers a cure-all prescription for women: "Simple, pure devotion to Christ. The balanced woman is not out to please some of the people all the time, or all of the people some of the time. She's not committed to please anyone at all . . . except Christ. Her strategy for living is to be simply, purely, passionately devoted to the Lord." It's this kind of godly advice you'll hear from Annie as she shares her insights on dealing with your emotions.

Florence Littauer lives with her husband, Fred, in Lake San Marcos, California, and is a well-known speaker, author of twenty books, and the founder of the organization C.L.A.S.S. (Christian Leaders and Speakers Seminars). Florence's mission for more than twenty years has been helping people understand themselves better. Whether it's through the leadership seminars she teaches or the books she writes, including her national best seller *Personality Plus* (Revell), Florence continually strives to encourage others to discover and appreciate the unique individuals God created them to be. "By looking at our inborn desires, our underlying needs, and our repressed emotions, our eyes will be opened and we will obtain some insight about who we really are. There is no magic wand to transform us into angels, but as we look at ourselves as God created us to be and come before Him in honesty, He will touch us with His healing power," she writes in her book *Your Personality Tree* (Word).

Florence and Fred have been married for forty years and together they travel around the world, ministering to the needs of others. Florence has given birth to four children, lost two of them to a regressive brain disease and adopted a son who is now in his thirties. These circumstances have presented her with a wide range of emotions that have increased her compassion for hurting people. Florence has a gift for encouraging and entertaining that she combines with her zest for life, her straightforward wisdom, and her caring concern for others. Florence's sense of humor and frank observations of human behavior are sure to lead you to many revelations about yourself and your emotions.

Completing our circle of contributors is the deeply reflective and creative *Luci Shaw*, known primarily as a poet and author of such collections as *Listen to the Green, Postcard from the Shore,* and *Writing the River* (Pinon Press) and *Polishing the Petoskey Stone* (Shaw Publishers). Her first book of prose, *God in the Dark* (Zondervan), met with critical acclaim. The book, based on her journals, probes with great transparency her emotional quest for understanding God's presence in the face of the death of her first husband, publisher Harold Shaw. *Life Path* (Multnomah), her workbook on journal-keeping, is the text for numerous journal workshops she leads across the continent to develop self-awareness and God-awareness. With spiritual depth and refreshing candor, Luci, a mother of five, brings to bear on the chapters in this book her own search for understanding of a woman's emotions. Today, Luci is remarried to John Hoyte and lives in California. She divides her time between her new home in Menlo Park, and the Pacific

Northwest, as writer-in-residence at Regent College, Vancouver.

As women, our emotional makeup is complex. Our emotions can frustrate us and set us back in our relationships with God and others. At the same time, though, the unique emotional sensitivities God has built into each of us can serve as stepping-stones to greater spiritual maturity.

As you read this book and begin to unravel the web of your own emotional makeup, may you discover new ways to bring your feelings and responses to others in line with God's will. And may you come to understand and appreciate the beauty and depth with which God created you.

Marian V. Liautaud and
Louise A. Ferrebee, Editors

PART ONE

RELATING TO OTHERS

FOR WOMEN, a direct correlation exists between how we feel about ourselves and how we relate to others. If our outlook on life is negative, chances are good that our attitude toward others will reflect negativity. Or if we harbor unresolved anger, we might see it surface as a sarcastic remark to our spouse or a friend.

Emotions like pessimism, anger, sadness, or guilt are not wrong in and of themselves. But when our feelings govern our actions, we soon find our emotions can lead to sin. For that reason, as growing Christians, it's essential that we examine how our emotions affect our relationships. And such self-examination undoubtedly requires a degree of honesty and humility, as Annie, Florence, and Luci have all modeled in the following chapters.

In this section, perhaps you will discover a pattern in your reactions to people when you feel angry. Maybe you'll begin to understand why your feelings are so easily hurt, or why those intense feelings of love you first felt for your spouse now seem a distant memory.

Whatever revelations you have, know that God stands ready to forgive and strengthen you when your emotions control your actions. But more than anything, know that He desires for each of us to bring our emotions under submission to Him in a way that will bring Him glory.

1

How Can I Develop an Optimistic Outlook Toward Life?

—Annie Chapman

TODAY, I CAN SAY I'm an optimistic person with a healthy mental outlook. That hasn't always been the case, though. Only by God's grace have I been able to change the way I view life.

Before I was saved, I was mired in negativity. I thought life was unfair and I expected little from it. I was a child given to depression. I would often sit on the hill above our farm and beg God to take my life. I also had physical problems—crippling arthritis. One doctor told me I'd be in a wheelchair before I was twenty-one.

Unfortunately, the unhealthy outlook that I had cultivated through the years didn't disappear the day I became a Christian. I discovered that putting a positive spin on life required intentional effort. It's much simpler for a doom-and-gloom person to continue viewing life pessimistically than it is to take the necessary steps toward developing a healthy mental outlook. But unless we begin to cultivate habits that help us see life optimistically, we will inevitably go through life feeling sorrowful.

Renew Your Mind

I realized the only way I could overcome my rotten attitude was if God overhauled my mind. Soon after I became a Christian, I would get up at 5:00 a.m. each morning to study the Scriptures. John 15:7 reads: "If you remain in me and my words remain in you, ask whatever you wish, and it will be given you." I asked God to renew my mind and make me a more positive person, and within six months I gradually began to see answers to my prayers.

There was a person (a non-family member) who had done me great harm. I hated this person and could hardly wait for God to condemn this individual to hell. My greatest need was to forgive this person. This was my greatest victory. Through God's work in my life I was able to forgive.

Scripture is an integral component for keeping our thinking and actions in line with God's. Hebrews 10:36 has become my life verse. "You need to persevere so that when you have done the will of God, you will receive what he has promised." Even though the circumstances of my life may press in on me and fill me with despair, I persevere because I know God will bless me for it.

Additionally, I'm reminded in 1 Corinthians 10:13 that "no temptation has seized you except what is common to man." Others have known my weaknesses and pain, and so by sharing my hurts with trusted friends I can gain an objective, realistic perspective on my life. With the help of a friend I can handle whatever hardships I might be facing.

Sometimes we get so caught up in the daily grind of life that we lose sight of what will last forever and what won't. Jeremiah 17:9 says, "The heart is deceitful above all things and beyond cure. . . ." Scripture and friends can serve as objective sounding boards to help remind us what is important and lasting in life.

WHAT REALLY COUNTS?

One of the quickest ways to gain perspective is to ask yourself, "Is this going to make a difference two years down the line?" Inevitably your answer will help clarify and redefine your priorities.

—Florence

I recently spoke with a mother of three (ages three, two, and eight months) who was about to lose her mind. She definitely had lost her positive outlook. I listened to her and tried to encourage her as best I could, yet nothing seemed to lift her load. Sometime later she called and shared a verse she had just found—Isaiah 40:11. "He tends his flock like a shepherd: He gathers the lambs in his arms and carries them close to his heart; he gently leads those that have young."

Her whole outlook changed as she realized that God saw her situation and He was there for her. Knowing the difference between the eternal and the temporal goes a long way toward maintaining a realistic, hopeful outlook.

Know Your Natural Bent

Even with the inherent positive outlook we have as Christians, as a result of the hope and power of Christ's resurrection, some of us seem predisposed to view our cup as half empty. Our approach to life is based in part on our personalities.

For instance, I'm a serious and introspective person. On the other hand, my husband, Steve, is laid-back and easygoing. While I value my thinker and worker side, I have seen over the years the need to lighten up and have more fun. I'm always the one telling the kids, "Keep your shoes clean," or "Don't tear your blue jeans," while Steve is the one playing with the kids, having a ball.

Lately, I've been joining in on their fun. When Steve takes the kids out on our boat, I try to go with them instead of staying home to catch up on laundry. I make an effort to meet regularly for dinner with some women friends. Inevitably, we spend the evening laughing and having fun. It takes a conscious effort on my part to kick back and relax, but the only way for me to maintain a positive outlook is if I'm achieving a balance between work and play.

On the Up-and-Up

Once you've considered how your personality affects your outlook and worked on bringing some balance to a naturally negative nature, take an honest look at your spiritual life. Is your relationship with the Lord on track? Is there any unconfessed sin in your life that may be keeping you from intimacy with God? Sometimes guilt is a good indicator of a relationship that is out of kilter. Like a fever, true guilt alerts us to some underlying problem. It's like that feeling of dread when you've succumbed to a sale and purchased another white blouse after you and your husband agreed not to spend any more money that month. Hiding the blouse in the closet becomes a point of guilt—you know eventually you'll have to tell your husband about it.

A word of caution, though. Guilt can be a tricky cue to follow. Too often it dominates our life unnecessarily and keeps us from living joyfully. If you have confessed your transgressions to the Lord, you can begin the day with a clean slate, confident that God has forgiven you. If guilt continues to plague you, it may be Satan's ploy to undermine the belief you have in God's power to forgive and cleanse. Remind yourself that you are forgiven and in right standing with God, and then begin to live as if you have a new lease on life.

Steve wrote a song, "The Secret Place,"[1] that describes how God comes to cleanse every part of our heart.

> My heart is like a house—
> One day I let the Savior in.
> And there are many rooms
> Where we would visit now and then.
> But one day He saw that room—
> I knew the day had come too soon.
> I said, "Jesus, I'm not ready
> For us to visit in that room.
>
> " 'Cause that's the place in my heart
> Where even I don't go.
> I have some things hidden there
> I don't want no one to know."
> But He handed me the key
> With tears of love on His face.
> He said, "I want to make you clean;
> let me go in your secret place."
>
> So I opened up the door,
> And as the two of us walked in
> I was so afraid.
> His light revealed my hidden sin,
> But when I think about that room now
> I'm not afraid anymore.
> 'Cause I know my hidden sin
> No longer hides behind that door.

---

[1]"The Secret Place" words and music my Steve Chapman. Copyright © 1981 by Shepherd's Fold Music (a Division of Star Song Communications/Administered by Gaither Copyright Management) and Career's Music. All rights reserved. Used by permission.

That was a place in my heart
Where even I wouldn't go.
I had some things hidden there
I didn't want no one to know.
But He handed me the key
With tears of love on His face.
He made me clean;
I let Him in my secret place.

Is there a place in your heart,
Where even you don't go?

Along with assessing your relationship with God, it also helps to take a look at your relationships with others. Are there negative emotions and sins that exist between you and a friend that are coloring your perspective on life? For instance, women sometimes covet each other's things. We want what our friend has. I definitely wrestled with negative feelings when I had to entertain some "rich folk" from our church. With my mind on how I was going to look and comparing my house to theirs, I was miserable. Only after confessing my covetousness to God as sin, and then asking Him to help me concentrate on meeting the needs of others, was I able to not only find a positive outlook but eventually gain a new and valued friend.

Stowing Old Baggage

Another step in discovering the source of your negative thinking is to consider the way your parents viewed life. Many of us inherit unhealthy habits while we're growing up and subconsciously transfer these traits into our adult lives. For instance, my mom is a worrier. Consequently, my natural tendency is to worry too. Since marrying Steve, though, I have learned to break my knee-jerk reflex to worry by learning to think more optimistically.

Steve is always putting me in situations where my "doomsday" attitudes come into play. He will take our son Nathan into the woods to hunt. If I allowed myself, I would entertain the most deadly of thoughts. However, when they return safely (and they always have, so far), they both are quick to point out the most positive aspects—the time spent together, the meaningful talks, and the freezer full of meat.

Breaking my old habit of seeing life from a more negative viewpoint hasn't been easy. For instance, last year Steve and Nathan went on a five-hundred-mile bike trip together. My natural reaction was to prohibit them from going just to alleviate my own worries over their safety. Rather than worry about their safety, I focused on thinking optimistically about all the benefits they would reap from traveling together.

---------- ✑ ----------

Besides examining the unhealthy thinking patterns we carried with us from childhood, we need to examine our speech patterns as well. I'm convinced that developing positive habits of speech is a key step in becoming a more optimistic person. How many times have you heard yourself say things like, "I can't lose weight," or, "I won't get that job"? Can't and won't are two of the most self-defeating words in the English language. They are nothing more than excuses that keep us from challenging ourselves to learn and grow.

In their book *Happiness Is a Choice* (Baker), Frank Minirth and Paul Meier offer this observation: "Whenever a non-Christian patient uses the word 'can't,' we let him get away with it because we believe him. A non-Christian without the power of God in his life really cannot choose righteous paths consistently."

As believers, we know that we "can do everything through him who gives [us] strength" (Philippians 4:13). By speaking more positively, we affirm our belief that all things are possible with Christ. And the more we focus on and verbalize what's right about life, the fuller our cup appears.

———————— ∽ ————————

All of us know people who seem to have a positive mental attitude no matter what the circumstances of their life. Though hard times and tough situations confront them, they face life with optimism. These people, whether they are Christians or not, truly believe and follow the basic premise of Minirth and Meier's book: happiness is a choice. Rather than buckle under the pressure of life, they choose to face their circumstances squarely and deal with problems positively.

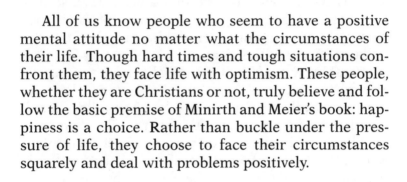

OPEN THE SAFETY VALVE

Laughter is like a safety valve. It lets you blow off a lot of energy that otherwise might get channeled into bitterness, disgust, anger, or frustration.
—*Luci*

As Christians we are mandated to make this same choice. That doesn't mean our life will be problem-free. And it doesn't mean we should wear a perpetual smile and deny the reality of our daily challenges. For instance, if I discover a lump in my breast I need to say, "This could be cancer, and I need to have it checked," instead of thinking, "God wouldn't let anything bad happen to me, so I don't need to worry about this."

The fact is bad things do happen to us. But as Christians, we have an inner peace and joy that says, "God is in control. Even though I don't like what is happening,

I know I can trust Him." When we live like this, those who know us will see that although we hurt at times, we have a place to bring our pain.

Optimists are often called idealists, as if their joy were based on some false sense of hope and they were not grounded in reality. Granted, there are those who deny reality and pretend that nothing bad ever happens to them. Joy like this is about as sturdy as whipped cream. Once the sun comes out and heats it up, it melts away.

A true healthy mental outlook, on the other hand, recognizes life's challenges, deals with them appropriately, and continues moving through life with a sense of peace that God is working to bring good out of difficult situations.

Make It Happen

1. We display a positive outlook in our speech, attitude, and actions toward others as well as our devotion to Christ. On a scale of 1–10, how would you rate yourself in each of these areas? How do you think others would rate you? In which areas does your positive spirit show? Which areas require attention?

2. As women, our outlook on life is intrinsically tied to how we feel about ourselves. If your physical appearance is keeping you from feeling good about the world around you, take action. Instead of complaining about the ten pounds that make all your clothes too tight, set a goal and implement a plan to shed the extra weight. Resolve to change the things you can and accept the things you either can't change or aren't willing to work at.

3. "Murmuring," that continual droning that kept the Israelites wandering in the desert for forty years, often seeps into our speech, subtly undermining our joy. Be aware of the times you complain, "This food's not good

enough," or "This hotel isn't nice enough," or "My house isn't big enough." Concentrate on erasing the "murmuring" that sabotages your enjoyment of life.

4. Read the story of Joseph, starting in Genesis 37. Though life was cruel and unfair to him, he didn't cave in with despair. Joseph knew God was watching over him and would someday deliver him from his trials. Have you allowed painful memories from your past to cloud your perspective about life? If so, seek God's forgiveness and His guidance in resolving the issues that keep you from enjoying a healthy mental outlook.

Are You a Negaholic?
Jane Johnson Struck

Life is like a glass of water, or so goes the well-worn analogy. Some people—the optimists of this world—view that glass as half full. They envision possibilities and opportunities. Others—the pessimists, or "negaholics"—view it as being half empty. They expect the worst so they won't be disappointed. Here are some ways to keep a healthy perspective.

Distance yourself emotionally. When I'm in the midst of one of my "the-sky-is-falling" episodes, it's difficult for me to assess whether or not I have a legitimate reason for concern or if I'm simply allowing myself to get carried away.

When a recent and unexpected biopsy triggered overwhelming fear in my life, the calm, objective counsel and prayers of a close friend became invaluable. She was able to listen to my fears—then gently point out how my "end-of-the-world" scenarios were based on speculation, not evidence.

Figure out your motive. "Ask yourself, *What am I avoiding by being panicky, negative, or fearful?*" says social worker Sheri Klinka. "Many times negative behavior becomes a way to avoid dealing with something the Holy Spirit may be convicting you to change."

Is your pessimism triggered by disappointment over relationships, anger with God, or fear of having to admit your own role in whatever problems you face? The sooner you own up to what lies behind the negaholism, the easier it becomes to develop a strategy for change.

Pinpoint the distortions. Lies about who God is and how He works can permeate our thoughts—and thoughts dictate our feelings. "Satan wants us to believe all sorts of things to damage our relationship to God," says Klinka. "If he can find ways to make us feel hopeless, defeated, or separated from God, he'll do it. And one way is through distorted thinking."

One woman I recently spoke with finds that journaling helps her sort through her thoughts and align her emotions with biblical truths. "I write it all out—my fears, my disappointments, my perceptions of a situation," she explains. "As I read back through it, I tell myself, *This is how I feel—now here is what the Bible has to say about the situation.* Then I compare my feelings to what Scripture has to say."

Switch the station to Scripture. Not long ago, my ten-year-old daughter had trouble falling asleep. That day her school had held a fire safety assembly.

"Mom," she called, her eyes filling with tears, "I can't fall asleep. I'm scared of a fire. What should we do?"

After I reassured her and prayed with her about her fear, she said more insistently, "I know the Lord heard us, but I still CAN'T stop thinking about a fire!"

"Pretend you're watching a scary movie on television," I told her. "You know what you would do? You'd switch the station to a happy program. You can decide to do the same thing with your thoughts."

We can combat negativism by making a conscious effort to reroute our thoughts. But far outweighing any "reprogramming" we can script for ourselves is the power in God's Word reminding us it's His Spirit that transforms our minds and hearts. While God's Word acknowledges, "As [a man] thinketh in his heart, so is he," (Proverbs 23:7, KJV) it also proclaims that it is "not by might nor by power, but by my Spirit" (Zechariah 4:6). When I indulge myself in pessimism, it's time for me to steep myself in prayer and in the promises and wisdom of the "author and finisher" of my faith.

—From *Today's Christian Woman* (November/December 1991)

2

What Is the Best Way to Respond When My Feelings Have Been Hurt?

—Florence Littauer

NO MATTER HOW thick-skinned we might be, we all experience hurt feelings from time to time. But before I offer some constructive ways to deal with hurt feelings, it helps to assess how sensitive each of us tends to be by nature.

Soon after Fred and I accepted the Lord, we became aware of the four basic personality types first taught by Greek philosopher and physician Hippocrates to his medical students more than two thousand years ago. This theory about personalities revolutionized our marriage. Upon learning of each other's unique personality traits, for the first time in fifteen years of marriage Fred and I began to accept each other as we were, not as we always had hoped the other would become.

Of course, we couldn't keep the concept to ourselves and soon invited ten couples to our home and began to share what we had learned. In spite of our limited background in the subject at that time, we saw marriages transformed. People who were clueless as to why they were having relationship problems suddenly saw themselves in a new light. Fred and I began speaking on the personalities to small groups, church meetings, and eventually conventions. I wrote several books on the topic, *Personality Plus* (Revell) and *Your Personality Tree* (Word), all on using this theory as a tool to help us examine and understand ourselves and learn to get along with difficult people. In Romans 12:18 Paul says, "If possible, so far as it depends on you, be at peace with all men" (NAS).

At the end of chapter two of this book is a copy of the Personality Profile that has been used by over one million people. Stop reading and take a few minutes to complete the profile. You should be able to determine your God-given personality and in the process better understand the degree to which you are naturally sensitive to other people's comments or actions. Scripture tells us to analyze ourselves. "But let a man examine himself" (1 Corinthians 11:28a, NAS). "But if we judged ourselves rightly, we should not be judged" (1 Corinthians 11:31, NAS). But the Bible doesn't give us a simple way to do this. Using the Personality Profile as a tool can help us evaluate ourselves objectively.

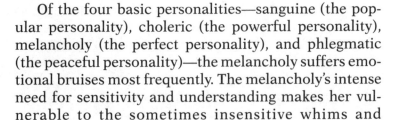

Of the four basic personalities—sanguine (the popular personality), choleric (the powerful personality), melancholy (the perfect personality), and phlegmatic (the peaceful personality)—the melancholy suffers emotional bruises most frequently. The melancholy's intense need for sensitivity and understanding makes her vulnerable to the sometimes insensitive whims and thoughtless words of the sanguine and choleric.

My oldest grandchild, Randy, is a very sensitive melancholy. One day I came to pick him up for a lunch date, and at the door was his sanguine younger brother Jonathan, bouncing up and down, begging to go with us. Now, from my perspective as a fellow sanguine, I knew it would be extra fun to take Jonathan along. I asked Randy, "Would it be okay if we took Jonathan just this once?" Randy's face dropped as he said, "Grammy, let's put it this way. If you take Jonathan, I'll stay home." Immediately I regretted my words. My invitation to include Jonathan wasn't meant to hurt Randy's feelings, yet it did. I needed to be more perceptive of his naturally sensitive nature.

Sometimes it's difficult for the sanguine and choleric to tune in to other people's feelings. The sanguine thrives on praise and only hears that which makes her feel good. You can say, "Nice hair today," and slip in, "Gee, you've put on weight," and it's likely the sanguine will be so thrilled with your compliment that she won't even hear the comment about the extra pounds. Conversely, if you tell a melancholy her hair looks nice today, she will wonder what was wrong with it yesterday.

The choleric is the least sensitive of all personality types. She won't even listen to the negatives because she knows she's right. She often has enough confidence in how right she is that it's unlikely you could say anything that would get to her. In fact, if you want cholerics to hear criticism, you almost have to take them by the shoulders and say, "Look at me and listen." Cholerics also love to prove how proficient they are, especially at handling crises. This definitely applies to me as I function half sanguine—let's have fun—and half choleric—I want to be in charge!

One time Fred told me, "You're the greatest emergency cook in the world. You can walk in at 5:00 P.M. and not have the foggiest notion what you're going to serve for dinner, and by 6 P.M. you've pulled together a beautiful meal." As he complimented me, I was thinking, "Isn't this wonderful. I'm so brilliant." Then came his punch line: "But could we have one meal a week that is not an emergency?"

The phlegmatic will appear unfazed by most comments but take heed—she internalizes everything. She may feel deeply hurt by some passing comment, but will spend her time mulling over whether or not it's worth acting on the criticism. Phlegmatics try to keep their emotions hidden. My mother, who was this type, often said, "I pride myself in the fact that no one ever knows what I'm really thinking." And we didn't!

Goodbye Distorted Perceptions

Once you've determined your personality type and how naturally sensitive you are to others, then there are three questions you need to ask yourself when you feel someone has hurt you.

First, "Is there any validity to what this person has said?" For example, if someone walks up to you and says, "You're wearing too much eyeliner," and you look in the mirror and discover you've got big black rims around your eyes, then there is some validity in that comment. This person may legitimately be trying to help you. However, if she were to say the same thing to you and you weren't wearing any eyeliner, then her statement is not valid and you should give it no further thought.

Unfortunately, most women straddle both sides of a negative comment. We think, "Maybe I do wear too much makeup." Then we call ten friends, ask what they think, and brood about their insights for days. Instead of accepting or rejecting a comment outright, we play the remark over and over in our minds until our perception of the truth is completely distorted by what others think.

In the public speaking classes I teach, everyone in each small group session gets a chance to critique one another after every speech. I tell my students to look over each comment. If ten people say, "Your dress is too drab, and it drains the color from your face," chances are there is some validity to the comment and you need to brighten up your image. But if nine out of ten people say, "You're a great speaker and you shouldn't change a thing," don't spend time agonizing over the one person who thinks you need a face-lift.

JUST THE WORDS

Occasionally my mother-in-law comes to watch the children while we're gone. She'll say, "I'd like to clean out your kitchen cabinets for you." I could easily take her offer as an insult concerning my housekeeping. Instead, I simply say, "Thank you, they desperately need to be cleaned." When I focus on the words spoken and don't look for a hidden meaning, I'm less likely to be hurt by someone's comments.

—Annie

Second, ask yourself, "How can I benefit from this criticism?" When someone comes up to me after a presentation and says, "Nice speech," I'll say, "What did I say today that helped you?" Or, "What changed you?" This gives me an opportunity to find out exactly where my presentations are strong and where they need work.

After I spoke at a women's retreat, I was mailed a large envelope full of evaluations. My favorite was, "Florence Littauer was unexpectedly exciting, which only goes to show that looks are deceiving." If I wished to brood over this I could wonder: *What was this lady expecting? Were my deceiving looks based on seeing me ten years ago, on a picture, or on how I looked at that moment?* I could phone people who were there and poll their opinions. Or I could run it through my mind, determine it didn't make any sense, and not let it bother me. I did the latter.

The final question to ask yourself is, "What is motivating this person to say what she did?" Scripture tells us in Philippians 4:8 that we are to see the best in others. We are to look at what's true, noble, just, pure, lovely, and of good report. "If anything is excellent or praiseworthy—think about such things" (v. 8b). Then why are so many Christians so critical? Usually, the more critical a person is the lower her self-worth. Emotionally healthy people don't need to put others down.

I remember one woman who came up to me after a seminar and snidely said, "I didn't agree at all with what you said today." Her comment stopped me in my tracks, but before I reacted negatively, I thought to myself, *Why is she being antagonistic toward me? What is she really trying to do?*

I've been in the public eye for a number of years, and I've learned some people just want to test your mettle. They want to prove that what you profess in public is a facade—that you aren't really a Christian. They want to cause you to fall off your pedestal so they can say, "She looks good on stage, but you should see how quickly she gets angry when you cross her!" Under these circumstances the best course of action is to do nothing in haste. Simply don't respond for a second. When this woman confronted me I swallowed and then said, "Well, thank you for listening. I don't blame you. If I'd heard someone say that, I would feel the same way." I knew fully well I had never said what she thought I had said. In fact, another woman overheard us and countered this woman in my defense.

Unfortunately, many people feel perfectly comfortable offering unsolicited advice or comments. Not long ago, a woman who attended my seminar came up to me later and said, "You look much younger on the platform." I responded, "I'll try to stay there as much as I can." When someone delivers a negative comment, I've learned to respond with humor, not sarcasm, whenever possible. It deflects many of the cruel remarks that would otherwise cut to the quick.

If you hurt easily, consider preparing a few standard comebacks to provide a buffer between your heart and the tears that too quickly well up in your eyes. Since you know their aim is to hurt or embarrass you, don't let them win. Some of my standbys are, "Thank you for your concern," "Thank you for noticing," or "Thank you for taking the time to come and speak to me." Try to have a few such statements in your head. If you have a prepared response, you'll be less likely to become unglued by another's uncaring comment. "Thank you" is the last thing they expect you to say, and it throws them off guard.

This Is How I Feel

When you sense someone is pushing you toward your sensitivity threshold, it's wise to say, "I don't want to talk about this now." Many of the women I talk with say that their husbands intentionally bring up sore subjects just to hurt or tease them. When your spouse does this, it's important to clearly and rationally tell him what effect his actions have on your emotions. For instance, if your spouse should continually compare you to his first wife, then say to him, "It really hurts me every time you mention your first wife." If you take the time to spell out exactly what behavior or words offend you and why, the better your spouse will be able and willing to change his hurtful behavior. Philippians 2:13 says, "God is always at work in you to make you willing and able to obey his good purpose" (TEV).

I'm not an overly sensitive person, but there are certain subjects that are emotionally threatening to me. Early in our marriage, Fred would tell me I talked too much. I'll admit this was true, but his assessment hurt. However, because I knew how important it was for me to listen at least as much as I talked, I made a concerted effort to change. In fact, I became so sensitive to this issue that I would barely utter a word at parties or at dinner with friends. Good things came out of my quietness—mainly Fred had an opportunity to talk, and I found out he really had something to say. But what bothered me was that Fred never seemed to notice I had changed. He would still say, in front of others, "Florence talks so much she wouldn't know what it was you said," despite the fact I'd been silent for an hour! He thought his comments were humorous, but I didn't take them as funny, especially when I'd tried so hard.

FLEXING SPIRITUAL MUSCLE

When Harold was alive he would listen to all the hurts and grievances I felt and in a sense protect me. After his death I was forced to deal with situations that made me feel bad. While this has been a difficult season of training for me, I feel I've developed spiritual and emotional muscles that I never knew I had. I'm now a stronger person in my own right.

—Luci

One night after a party, I asked Fred, "What do you remember me talking about tonight?"

"Well, I don't remember that you said anything," he replied.

"That's true, I didn't. I made sure I didn't. However, when we left you told everybody I always talk too much, and that's not true."

It finally dawned on him that I had changed my behavior and didn't talk as much as I used to. It was as though I had to wean Fred from the habit of teasing me about my talking.

As Christians we're told to turn the other cheek when someone hurts us. Certainly, this is an appropriate response in many situations. However, we are not commanded to tolerate brow-beating or to serve as doormats for others to walk all over. If someone you live with or frequently see hurts you, you have a right to let them know so they don't continue in their sin.

God created each of us with a unique measure of sensitivity. No matter how emotionally tough we appear to be, each of us has areas where we are vulnerable. Some channel this gift of great sensitivity outward in the form of compassion and feeling for others. Because I have lost two children, I have a heart for grieving mothers. Because my husband was molested as a child, he is willing to spend many hours each week ministering to those in emotional pain.

Others, though, keep their sensitivity focused inward, causing them to harbor many hurts and wounds imposed by the perceived callousness of those around them. While all of us are hurt from time to time by the thoughtless words and actions of others, more often than not it is pride and self-centeredness that turns an off-the-cuff, innocent remark into grounds for a pity-party. By being aware of the areas where we feel most vulnerable emotionally and then committing these to God, we can begin to bolster ourselves emotionally.

What can we do to help others? Once we understand and accept the differences in other people, we can learn how to get along with them better and how to meet their emotional needs. The sanguine is close to desperate for attention and approval. The choleric needs appreciation for the work he or she has done. The melancholic needs sensitivity and periods of silence. The phlegmatic needs a sense of stability and peace. When we realize that we all have different emotional needs, we can begin to treat others in a way that will bless them and not irritate them.

In Romans 12, Paul, apparently a strong choleric, emphasizes personal differences and admonishes us to "rejoice with those who rejoice; mourn with those who mourn. Live in harmony with one another" (vv. 15–16). It has helped me to learn that the Lord wants me to accept people as they are, live in harmony with them, and help meet their emotional needs. "Do not be proud," Paul continues, "but be willing to associate with people of low position" (v. 16), (or perhaps people who aren't like me).

"Let us therefore make every effort to do what leads to peace and to mutual edification. Do not destroy the work of God for the sake of food," says Paul in Romans 14:19–20, or for the sake of my trivial personality differences or desires. Paul wants so much for Christians to live in peace, to get along with each other, that he continues to emphasize this need for a spirit of unity. "Accept one another, then, just as Christ accepted you, in order to bring praise to God" (Romans 15:7).

As we look first at our own personal sensitivities and then at the emotional needs of others, we should be able to realize that Christ has accepted us just as we are. Can't we then adjust to the differences in others?

Make It Happen

1. Complete the Personality Profile at the end of this chapter. What personality type are you? Are you especially prone to hurt feelings? If so, celebrate the fact that you have a unique sensitivity to life and people. Seek out ways to channel your deep ability to feel where compassion is most needed in your family, church, or community.

2. Think through the areas that make you feel emotionally threatened. What makes you sensitive to criticism in these areas? Often at the root of our hurt feelings is an unconfessed sin, like pride or anger or hidden pain of the past that needs to be faced. Ask the Lord to search your heart and bring to light any area where you need His forgiveness or His healing touch.

3. If you live or die by the approval of others, meditate on Psalm 139. Remember that God made you who you are. He gave you His stamp of approval before you ever came to be.

Personality Profile
Florence Littauer

DIRECTIONS—In each of the rows of four words across on the next page, place an X in front of the one word that most often applies to you. If you cannot decide which word best fits you, then think of yourself when you were a child or ask your spouse or a friend who knows you well.

Continue through all forty lines. Be sure to place one X on each horizontal line. Reading the definition of each word on the following pages will help you make your choices.

STRENGTHS

1.	__Animated	__Adventurous	__Analytical	__Adaptable
2.	__Persistent	__Playful	__Persuasive	__Peaceful
3.	__Submissive	__Self-sacrificing	__Sociable	__Strong-willed
4.	__Considerate	__Controlled	__Competitive	__Convincing
5.	__Refreshing	__Respectful	__Reserved	__Resourceful
6.	__Satisfied	__Sensitive	__Self-reliant	__Spirited
7.	__Planner	__Patient	__Positive	__Promoter
8.	__Sure	__Spontaneous	__Scheduled	__Shy
9.	__Orderly	__Obliging	__Outspoken	__Optimistic
10.	__Friendly	__Faithful	__Funny	__Forceful
11.	__Daring	__Delightful	__Diplomatic	__Detailed
12.	__Cheerful	__Consistent	__Cultured	__Confident
13.	__Idealistic	__Independent	__Inoffensive	__Inspiring
14.	__Demonstrative	__Decisive	__Dry humor	__Deep
15.	__Mediator	__Musical	__Mover	__Mixes easily
16.	__Thoughtful	__Tenacious	__Talker	__Tolerant
17.	__Listener	__Loyal	__Leader	__Lively
18.	__Contented	__Chief	__Chartmaker	__Cute
19.	__Perfectionist	__Permissive	__Productive	__Popular
20.	__Bouncy	__Bold	__Behaved	__Balanced

WEAKNESSES

21.	__Brassy	__Bossy	__Bashful	__Blank
22.	__Undisciplined	__Unsympathetic	__Unenthusiastic	__Unforgiving
23.	__Reticent	__Resentful	__Resistant	__Repetitious
24.	__Fussy	__Fearful	__Forgetful	__Frank
25.	__Impatient	__Insecure	__Indecisive	__Interrupts
26.	__Unpopular	__Uninvolved	__Unpredictable	__Unaffectionate
27.	__Headstrong	__Haphazard	__Hard to please	__Hesitant
28.	__Plain	__Pessimistic	__Proud	__Permissive
29.	__Angered easily	__Aimless	__Argumentative	__Alienated
30.	__Naive	__Negative attitude	__Nervy	__Nonchalant
31.	__Worrier	__Withdrawn	__Workaholic	__Wants credit
32.	__Too sensitive	__Tactless	__Timid	__Talkative
33.	__Doubtful	__Disorganized	__Domineering	__Depressed
34.	__Inconsistent	__Introvert	__Intolerant	__Indifferent
35.	__Messy	__Moody	__Mumbles	__Manipulative
36.	__Slow	__Stubborn	__Show-off	__Skeptical
37.	__Loner	__Lord over	__Lazy	__Loud
38.	__Sluggish	__Suspicious	__Short-tempered	__Scatterbrained
39.	__Revengeful	__Restless	__Reluctant	__Rash
40.	__Compromising	__Critical	__Crafty	__Changeable

Now transfer all your marks to the personality scoring sheet on page 54 and add up your totals.

PERSONALITY TEST WORD DEFINITIONS

STRENGTHS

1. **Animated** Full of life, lively use of hand, arm, and face gestures.
   Adventurous One who will take on new and daring enterprises with a need to master them.
   Analytical One who is constantly in the process of analyzing people, places, or things.
   Adaptable One who easily adapts to any situation.

2. **Persistent** Refusing to let go, insistently repetitive or continuous, can't drop it.
   Playful Full of fun and good humor.
   Persuasive One who persuades through logic and fact rather than charm.
   Peaceful One who seems undisturbed and tranquil and who retreats from any form of strife.

3. **Submissive** One who easily submits to any other's point of view or desire. This person has little need to assert his own view or opinion.
   Self-sacrificing One who constantly sacrifices his/her own personal well-being for the sake of or to meet the needs of others.
   Sociable This sociable refers to one who sees being with others as an opportunity to be cute and entertaining. If you are one who enjoys social gatherings as a challenge or business opportunity, then do not check this word.
   Strong-willed One who is determined to have his/her own way.

4. **Considerate** Having regard for the needs and feelings of others.
   Controlled One who has emotional feelings but doesn't display them.
   Competitive One who turns every situation, happening, or game into an arena for competition. This person always plays to win!
   Convincing This person can convince you of anything through the sheer charm of his/her personality. Facts are unimportant.

5. **Refreshing** One who renews and stimulates or pleasantly lifts spirits.
   Respectful One who treats others with deference, honor, and esteem.
   Reserved Self-restraint in expression of emotion or enthusiasm.
   Resourceful One who is able to act quickly and effectively in virtually all situations.

6. **Satisfied** A person who easily accepts any circumstance or situation.
   Sensitive This person is intensely sensitive to self and others.

Self-reliant An independent person who can fully rely on his/her own capabilities, judgment, and resources.

Spirited One who is full of life and excitement.

7. **Planner** One who prefers to work out a detailed arrangement beforehand, for the accomplishment of a project or goal. This person much prefers involvement with the planning stages and the finished product rather than the carrying out of the task.

   Patient One who is unmoved by delay—calm and tolerant.

   Positive Characterized by certainty and assurance.

   Promoter One who can compel others to go along, join, or invest through the sheer charm of his/her own personality.

8. **Sure** One who is confident, not hesitating or wavering.

   Spontaneous One who prefers all of life to be impulsive, unpremeditated activity. This person feels restricted by plans.

   Scheduled This person is controlled by his/her schedule and gets very upset if that schedule is interrupted. There is another type of person who uses a schedule to stay organized, but is not controlled by the schedule. If the second description is you, do not check this word.

   Shy Quiet, doesn't easily initiate a conversation.

9. **Orderly** A person who has a methodical, systematic arrangement of things.

   Obliging Accommodating. One who is quick to do it another's way.

   Outspoken One who speaks frankly and without reserve.

   Optimistic This optimist is an almost childlike, dreamer type of optimist.

10. **Friendly** This person is a responder to friendliness rather than an initiator. While he/she seldom starts a conversation, he/she responds with great warmth and enjoys the exchange.

    Faithful Consistently reliable. Steadfast, loyal, and devoted sometimes beyond reason.

    Funny This person has an innate humor that can make virtually any story a funny one and is a remarkable joke teller. If you have dry humor, do not check this word.

    Forceful A commanding personality. One would hesitate to take a stand against this person.

11. **Daring** One who is willing to take risks; fearless, bold.

    Delightful A person who is greatly pleasing, fun to be with.

    Diplomatic One who deals with people both tactfully and sensitively.

    Detailed A person who prefers working with the minute or fields that require detail work such as math, research, accounting, carving, art, graphics, etc.

12. **Cheerful** Consistently being in good spirits and promoting cheer.
    Consistent A person who is agreeable, compatible, not contradictory.
    Cultured One whose interests involve both intellectual and artistic pursuits, such as theater, symphony, ballet, etc.
    Confident One who is self-assured and/or certain of success.

13. **Idealistic** One who visualizes things in an ideal or perfect form, and has a need to measure up to that standard.
    Independent One who is self-sufficient, self-supporting, self-confident, and seems to have little need of help.
    Inoffensive A person who never causes offense; pleasant, unobjectionable, harmless.
    Inspiring One who encourages others to work, join, or be involved. There is another personality that is deeply inspirational and has a need to bring life-changing inspiration. If you are the latter, do not check this word.

14. **Demonstrative** One who openly expresses emotion, especially affection. This person doesn't hesitate to touch others while speaking to them.
    Decisive A person with quick, conclusive, decision-making ability.
    Dry humor One who exhibits dry wit, usually one-liners which can be sarcastic in nature, but very humorous.
    Deep A person who is intense and often introspective with a distaste for surface conversation and pursuits.

15. **Mediator** A person who consistently finds him/herself in the role of reconciling differences in order to avoid conflict.
    Musical One who either participates in or has an intense appreciation for music. This type of musical would not include those who find it fun to sing or play. The latter would be a different personality that enjoys being an entertainer rather than one who is deeply committed to music as an art form.
    Mover One who is so driven by a need to be productive that he/she finds it difficult to sit still.
    Mixes easily One who loves a party and can't wait to meet everyone in the room.

16. **Thoughtful** A considerate person who remembers special occasions and is quick to make a kind gesture.
    Tenacious One who holds on firmly, stubbornly, and won't let go till the goal is accomplished.
    Talker A person who is constantly talking, generally telling funny stories and entertaining everyone around him/her. There is another compulsive talker who is a nervous talker and feels the need to fill the silence in order to make others comfortable. This is not the entertaining talker we are describing here.

Tolerant One who easily accepts the thoughts and ways of others without the need to disagree with or change them.

17. **Listener** One who always seems willing to listen.

    Loyal Faithful to a person, ideal, or job. This person is sometimes loyal beyond reason and to his/her own detriment.

    Leader A person who is a born leader. This is not one who rises to the occasion because he/she can lead, but one who is driven to lead and finds it very difficult to believe anyone else can do the job.

    Lively Full of life, vigorous, energetic.

18. **Contented** One who is easily satisfied with what he/she has.

    Chief A person who commands leadership.

    Chartmaker One who enjoys either graphs, charts, or lists.

    Cute Bubbly-beauty, cutie, precious, diminutive.

19. **Perfectionist** One who desires perfection but not necessarily in every area of life.

    Permissive This person is permissive with employees, friends, and children in order to avoid conflict.

    Productive One who must constantly be working and/or producing. This person finds it very difficult to rest.

    Popular One who is the life of the party and therefore is much desired as a party guest.

20. **Bouncy** A bubbly, lively personality.

    Bold Fearless, daring, forward.

    Behaved One who consistently desires to conduct him/herself within the realm of what is proper.

    Balanced Stable, middle-of-the-road personality, without extremes.

WEAKNESSES

21. **Brassy** One who is showy, flashy, comes on strong.

    Bossy Commanding, domineering, overbearing. (Do not relate this to the raising of children. All mothers seem bossy and domineering. Rather, think of adult relationships.)

    Bashful One who shrinks from notice, resulting from self-consciousness.

    Blank A person who shows little facial expression or emotion.

22. **Undisciplined** A person whose lack of discipline permeates virtually every area of his/her life.

    Unsympathetic One who finds it difficult to relate to the problems or hurts of others.

    Unenthusiastic A person who finds it hard to get excited or feel enthusiasm.

Unforgiving One who has difficulty forgiving or forgetting a hurt or injustice done to him/her. This individual may find it hard to release a grudge.

23. **Reticent** One who is unwilling or struggles against getting involved.

    Resentful This person easily feels resentment as a result of real or imagined offenses.

    Resistant One who strives, works against, or resists accepting any other way but his/her own.

    Repetitious This person retells stories and incidents to entertain you without realizing he/she has already told the story several times before. This is not a question so much of forgetfulness, as it is of constantly needing something to say.

24. **Fussy** One who is insistent over petty matters or details, calling for great attention to trivial details.

    Fearful One who often experiences feelings of fear, apprehension, or anxiousness.

    Forgetful This person is forgetful because it isn't fun to remember. His/her forgetfulness is tied to a lack of discipline. There is another personality that is more like the absentminded professor. This person tends to be off in another world and only remembers what he/she chooses to remember. If you are the latter, do not check this word.

    Frank One who is straightforward, outspoken, and doesn't mind telling you exactly what he/she thinks.

25. **Impatient** A person who finds it difficult to endure irritation or wait patiently.

    Insecure One who is apprehensive or lacks confidence.

    Indecisive This person finds it difficult to make a decision at all. There is another personality that labors long over each decision in order to make the perfect one. If you are the latter, do not check this word.

    Interrupts This person interrupts because he/she is afraid of forgetting the wonderful thing he/she has to say if another is allowed to finish. This person is more of a talker than a listener.

26. **Unpopular** A person whose intensity and demand for perfection can push others away.

    Uninvolved One who has no desire to become involved in clubs, groups, or people activities.

    Unpredictable This person may be ecstatic one moment and blue the next, willing to help and then disappear, promising to come and then forgetting to show up.

    Unaffectionate One who finds it difficult to verbally or physically demonstrate affection openly.

27. **Headstrong** One who insists on having his/her own way.

    Haphazard One who has no consistent way of doing things.

    Hard to please A person whose standards are set so high that it is difficult to ever please him/her.

    Hesitant This person is slow to get moving and hard to get involved.

28. **Plain** A middle-of-the-road personality without highs or lows and showing little if any emotion.

    Pessimistic This person, while hoping for the best, generally sees the down side of a situation first.

    Proud One with great self-esteem who sees him/herself as always right and the best person for the job.

    Permissive This person allows others (including children) to do as they please in order to keep from being disliked.

29. **Angered easily** One who has a childlike flash in the pan temper that expresses itself in a child's tantrum style. It is over and forgotten almost instantly.

    Aimless A person who is not a goal-setter and has little desire to be one.

    Argumentative One who incites arguments generally because he/she is determined to be right no matter what the situation may be.

    Alienated A person who easily feels estranged from others, often because of insecurity or fear that others don't really enjoy his/her company.

30. **Naive** A simple and childlike perspective, lacking sophistication or worldliness. This is not be confused with uninformed. There is another personality that is so consumed with his/her own particular field of interest that he/she simply could not care less what is going on outside of that sphere. If you are the latter, do not check this word.

    Negative One whose attitude is seldom positive and who is often able to see only the down or dark side of each situation.

    Nervy Full of confidence, fortitude, and sheer guts.

    Nonchalant Easy-going, unconcerned, indifferent.

31. **Worrier** One who consistently feels uncertain or troubled.

    Withdrawn A person who pulls back to him/herself and needs a great deal of alone or isolation time.

    Workaholic This is one of two workaholic personalities. This particular one is an aggressive goal-setter who must be constantly productive and feels very guilty when resting. This workaholic is not driven by a need for perfection or completion but by a need for accomplishment and reward.

    Wants credit One who is almost dysfunctional without the credit or approval of others. As an entertainer, this person feeds on the applause, laughter, and/or acceptance of an audience.

32. **Too sensitive** One who is overly sensitive and introspective.

    Tactless A person who can sometimes express him/herself in a somewhat offensive and inconsiderate way.

    Timid One who shrinks from difficult situations.

    Talkative A compulsive talker who finds it difficult to listen. Again, this is an entertaining talker and not a nervous talker.

33. **Doubtful** A person who is full of doubts, uncertain.

    Disorganized One whose lack of organizational ability touches virtually every area of life.

    Domineering One who compulsively takes control of situations and/or people. Do not consider the mothering role. All mothers are somewhat domineering.

    Depressed A person who struggles with bouts of depression on a fairly consistent basis.

34. **Inconsistent** Erratic, contradictory, illogical.

    Introvert A person whose thoughts and interests are directed inward. One who lives within him/herself.

    Intolerant One who appears unable to withstand or accept another's attitudes, point of view, or way of doing things.

    Indifferent A person to whom most things don't matter one way or the other.

35. **Messy** This person is messy because it isn't fun to discipline him/herself to clean. The mess is hardly noticed. There is another personality that gets messy when depressed, and yet another that is messy because it takes too much energy to do the cleaning.

    Moody One who easily slips into moods. This person doesn't get very high emotionally, but does experience very low lows.

    Mumbles This person may mumble quietly under the breath when pushed. This is a passive display of anger.

    Manipulative One who influences or manages shrewdly or deviously for one's own advantage. One who will find a way to get his/her own way.

36. **Slow** One who is slow-moving, easy-going.

    Stubborn A person who is determined to exert his/her own will. Not easily persuaded; obstinate.

    Show-off One who needs to be the center of attention.

    Skeptical Disbelieving, questioning the motive behind the words.

37. **Loner** One who requires a lot of alone time and tends to avoid other people.

    Lord over A person who doesn't hesitate to let you know that he/she is right or has won.

Lazy One who evaluates work or activity in terms of how much energy it will take.

Loud A person whose laugh or voice can be heard above others in the room.

38. **Sluggish** Slow to get started.

    Suspicious One who tends to suspect or distrust.

    Short-tempered One who has a demanding impatience-based anger and a very short fuse. This type of anger is expressed when others are not moving fast enough or have not completed what they have been asked to do.

    Scatterbrained A person lacking the power of concentration or attention. Flighty.

39. **Revengeful** One who knowingly or otherwise holds a grudge and punishes the offender, often by subtly withholding friendship or affection.

    Restless A person who likes constant new activity because it isn't fun to do the same things all the time.

    Reluctant One who is unwilling or struggles against getting involved.

    Rash One who may act hastily, without thinking things through, generally because of impatience.

40. **Compromising** A person who will often compromise, even when he/she is right, in order to avoid conflict.

    Critical One who constantly evaluates and makes judgments. Example: One who is critical might see someone coming down the street and within seconds might try to evaluate their cleanliness or lack of it, of intelligence or lack of it, style of clothing or lack of it, physical attractiveness or lack of it, and the list goes on. This person constantly analyzes and critiques, sometimes without realizing he/she is doing so.

    Crafty Shrewd, one who can always find a way to get to the desired end.

    Changeable A person with a childlike, short attention span that needs a lot of change and variety to keep from getting bored.

PERSONALITY SCORING SHEET
STRENGTHS

	Popular **SANGUINE**	Powerful **CHOLERIC**	Perfect **MELANCHOLY**	Peaceful **PHLEGMATIC**
1.	__Animated	__Adventurous	__Analytical	__Adaptable
2.	__Playful	__Persuasive	__Persistent	__Peaceful
3.	__Sociable	__Strong-willed	__Self-sacrificing	__Submissive
4.	__Convincing	__Competitive	__Considerate	__Controlled
5.	__Refreshing	__Resourceful	__Respectful	__Reserved
6.	__Spirited	__Self-reliant	__Sensitive	__Satisfied
7.	__Promoter	__Positive	__Planner	__Patient
8.	__Spontaneous	__Sure	__Scheduled	__Shy
9.	__Optimistic	__Outspoken	__Orderly	__Obliging
10.	__Funny	__Forceful	__Faithful	__Friendly
11.	__Delightful	__Daring	__Detailed	__Diplomatic
12.	__Cheerful	__Confident	__Cultured	__Consistent
13.	__Inspiring	__Independent	__Idealistic	__Inoffensive
14.	__Demonstrative	__Decisive	__Deep	__Dry Humor
15.	__Mixes easily	__Mover	__Musical	__Mediator
16.	__Talker	__Tenacious	__Thoughtful	__Tolerant
17.	__Lively	__Leader	__Loyal	__Listener
18.	__Cute	__Chief	__Chartmaker	__Contented
19.	__Popular	__Productive	__Perfectionist	__Permissive
20.	__Bouncy	__Bold	__Behaved	__Balanced
Totals	_____	_____	_____	_____

WEAKNESSES

21.	__Brassy	__Bossy	__Bashful	__Blank
22.	__Undisciplined	__Unsympathetic	__Unforgiving	__Unenthusiastic
23.	__Repetitious	__Resistant	__Resentful	__Reticent
24.	__Forgetful	__Frank	__Fussy	__Fearful
25.	__Interrupts	__Impatient	__Insecure	__Indecisive
26.	__Unpredictable	__Unaffectionate	__Unpopular	__Uninvolved
27.	__Haphazard	__Headstrong	__Hard-to-please	__Hesitant
28.	__Permissive	__Proud	__Pessimistic	__Plain
29.	__Angered easily	__Argumentative	__Alienated	__Aimless
30.	__Naive	__Nervy	__Negative attitude	__Nonchalant
31.	__Wants credit	__Workaholic	__Withdrawn	__Worrier
32.	__Talkative	__Tactless	__Too sensitive	__Timid
33.	__Disorganized	__Domineering	__Depressed	__Doubtful
34.	__Inconsistent	__Intolerant	__Introvert	__Indifferent
35.	__Messy	__Manipulative	__Moody	__Mumbles
36.	__Show-off	__Stubborn	__Skeptical	__Slow
37.	__Loud	__Lord over	__Loner	__Lazy
38.	__Scatterbrained	__Short-tempered	__Suspicious	__Sluggish
39.	__Restless	__Rash	__Revengeful	__Reluctant
40.	__Changeable	__Crafty	__Critical	__Compromising
Totals	_____	_____	_____	_____
Combined Totals	_____	_____	_____	_____

PERSONALITY STRENGTHS

	SANGUINE Popular *THE TALKER*	CHOLERIC Powerful *THE WORKER*	MELANCHOLY Perfect *THE THINKER*	PHLEGMATIC Peaceful *THE WATCHER*
E M O T I O N S	Appealing personality Talkative, storyteller Life-of-the-party Good sense of humor Memory for color Physically holds onto listener Emotional and demonstrative Enthusiastic and expressive Cheerful and bubbling over Curious Good on stage Wide-eyed and innocent Lives in the present Changeable disposition Sincere at heart Always a child	Born leader Dynamic and active Compulsive need for change Must correct wrongs Strong-willed and decisive Unemotional Not easily discouraged Independent and self-sufficient Exudes confidence Can run anything	Deep and thoughtful Analytical Serious and purposeful Talented and creative Artistic or musical Philosophical and poetic Appreciative of beauty Sensitive to others Self-sacrificing Conscientious Idealistic	Low-key personality Easygoing and relaxed Calm, cool, and collected Patient, well-balanced Consistent life Quiet, but witty Sympathetic and kind Keeps emotions hidden Happily reconciled to life All-purpose person
W O R K	Volunteers for jobs Thinks up new activities Looks great on the surface Creative and colorful Has energy and enthusiasm Starts in a flashy way Inspires others to join Charms others to work	Goal-oriented Sees the whole picture Organizes well Seeks practical solutions Moves quickly to action Delegates work Insists on production Makes the goal Stimulates activity Thrives on opposition	Schedule-oriented Perfectionist, high standards Detail-conscious Persistent and thorough Orderly and organized Neat and tidy Economical Sees the problems Finds creative solutions Needs to finish what he starts Likes charts, graphs, figures, lists	Competent and steady Peaceful and agreeable Has administrative ability Mediates problems Avoids conflicts Good under pressure Finds the easy way
F R I E N D S	Makes friends easily Loves people Thrives on compliments Seems exciting Envied by others Doesn't hold grudges Apologizes quickly Prevents dull moments Likes spontaneous activities	Has little need for friends Will work for group activity Will lead and organize Is usually right Excels in emergencies	Makes friends cautiously Content to stay in background Avoids causing attention Faithful and devoted Will listen to complaints Can solve others' problems Deep concern for other people Moved to tears with compassion Seeks ideal mate	Easy to get along with Pleasant and enjoyable Inoffensive Good listener Dry sense of humor Enjoys watching people Has many friends Has compassion and concern

PERSONALITY WEAKNESSES

	SANGUINE Popular *THE TALKER*	CHOLERIC Powerful *THE WORKER*	MELANCHOLY Perfect *THE THINKER*	PHLEGMATIC Peaceful *THE WATCHER*
E M O T I O N S	Compulsive talker Exaggerates and elaborates Dwells on trivia Can't remember names Scares others off Too happy for some Has restless energy Egotistical Blusters and complains Naive, gets taken in Has loud voice and laugh Controlled by circumstances Gets angry easily Seems phony to some Never grows up	Bossy Impatient Quick-tempered Can't relax Too impetuous Enjoys controversy & arguments Won't give up when losing Comes on too strong Inflexible Is not complimentary Dislikes tears and emotions Is unsympathetic	Remembers the negatives Moody and depressed Enjoys being hurt Has false humility Off in another world Low self-image Has selective hearing Self-centered Too introspective Guilt feelings Persecution complex Tends to hypochondria	Unenthusiastic Fearful and worried Indecisive Avoids responsibility Quiet will of iron Selfish Too shy and reticent Too compromising Self-righteous
W O R K	Would rather talk Forgets obligations Doesn't follow through Confidence fades fast Undisciplined Priorities out of order Decides by feelings Easily distracted Wastes time talking	Little tolerance for mistakes Doesn't analyze details Bored by trivia May make rash decisions May be rude or tactless Manipulates people Demanding of others End justifies the means Work may become his god Demands loyalty in the ranks	Not people-oriented Depressed over imperfections Chooses difficult work Hesitant to start projects Spends too much time planning Prefers analysis to work Self-deprecating Hard to please Standards often too high Deep need for approval	Not goal-oriented Lacks self-motivation Hard to get moving Resents being pushed Lazy and careless Discourages others Would rather watch
F R I E N D S	Hates to be alone Needs to be on center stage Wants to be popular Looks for credit Dominates conversations Interrupts and doesn't listen Answers for others Fickle and forgetful Makes excuses Repeats stories	Tends to use people Dominates others Decides for others Knows everything Can do everything better Is too independent Possessive of friends and mate Can't say "I'm sorry" May be right, but unpopular	Lives through others Insecure socially Withdrawn and remote Critical of others Holds back affection Dislikes those in opposition Suspicious of people Antagonistic and vengeful Unforgiving Full of contradictions Skeptical of compliments	Dampens enthusiasm Stays uninvolved Is not exciting Indifferent to plans Judges others Sarcastic and teasing Resists change

Normal Healthy Patterns

Natural combinations of birth personalities are: Sanguine/Choleric, Choleric/Melancholy, Phlegmatic/Sanguine, and Melancholy/Phlegmatic.

One of the two will be your dominant and the other will be your secondary. Most everyone has a dominant and a secondary, but the numbers may vary greatly. For example, 32 Choleric with 8 Melancholy would be described as a very strong Choleric with some Melancholy traits.

However, it is also quite possible to have more evenly balanced scores in two columns. One or two checks in the remaining two columns can generally be ignored as insignificant. Any test such as this can be assumed to have a ten percent margin of error, for the words simply represent how you perceive yourself. Normal healthy patterns are usually characterized by similar and balancing scores of strengths and weaknesses in any single column.

Unnatural Combinations

There are two combinations, though often seen, that are not natural: (1) Sanguine/Melancholy, and (2) Choleric/Phlegmatic. Either of these two appearing on the scoring sheet in significant numbers is evidence of a "personality mask" as they are diametrically opposite and are not natural birth personality combinations. They are inevitably (1) the result of outside forces working in our life to make us conform to someone else's concept of who we should be, or (2) put on in childhood to survive in a difficult or dysfunctional family living situation.

Causes of Masking

1. *A domineering parent* in childhood, constantly requiring the child to conform to the personality they

want the child to have. A Melancholy/Choleric parent, for example, tries to make a spontaneous sanguine child into a meticulously neat melancholy.

2. An *alcoholic parent* in childhood, forcing unnatural pressures for the child to perform or contribute to the household, often assuming parental roles not natural for a child or his God-given birth personality.

3. Strong *rejection feelings* in childhood. A child who does not feel the love of one parent, or especially true if it is both parents. The child will often try to "be perfect" for the unloving parent in order to win the love, attention, and approval so eagerly craved and needed by every child.

4. Any form of *emotional or physical abuse* will quickly teach the child that the only way to hope to stop the harsh treatment is to conform to the demands of the abusing parent.

5. *Childhood sexual interference* or violation is inevitably a cause of masking, particularly when perpetrated by a parent or a person playing the parental role. The child subconsciously rationalizes that maybe if I would just be good enough, they would leave me alone. This is especially true when the knowledge of these childhood experiences has been completely suppressed and unknown in adult life. This mask may be seen in a person with a high score in melancholy weaknesses, without a comparable number of strengths; or in a person with a high number of sanguine strengths without balancing weaknesses.

6. *Single-Parent Home.* A child raised in a single-parent home, especially a firstborn, may often be required to fulfill some of the roles of the absent parent. When these functions are not consistent with the child's natural personality, he is apt to put on a mask which he generally continues wearing in adult life.

7. *Birth Order.* Young parents frequently pour on their first child an overzealous energy to make that child

conform to their concept of what he/she should be. When this does not coincide with the natural personality, masking may result.

8. *Legalistic Religious Home.* Intensely regulatory standards where appearance and conformance are required will often throttle a child's natural personality and zest for living, as the child learns to conform to legalism rather than respond to love.

9. A *domineering and controlling spouse* in adult life can have a similar effect as a domineering parent in childhood. This is most often seen, for example, when a strong Melancholy/Choleric husband tries to change a sanguine wife into his concept of what his wife should be, and how she should act. After a period of such control she may perceive herself to be Melancholy/Phlegmatic, when in fact it is nothing more than a mask to cope or survive in the marriage.

10. *Adult abuse or rejection* in marriage will often have the same effect in distorting the natural personality, as the lonely or hurting person puts on a mask and simply gives up.

Combination of Three

Any combination of three personalities indicates one must be a mask, for the reasons described above. Generally, the "center" of the three is the natural and one of the "ends" is a mask. For example, for a person scoring relatively evenly in Sanguine/Choleric/Melancholy, the Choleric is generally the natural and either the Sanguine or the Melancholy is the mask, as you were not born with both. You should try to determine which is the real and which is the mask.

Frequently a person who knows you well can objectively review your two columns in question and help you better select the word that they feel describes you better. Or, you can think back to how you felt, or would have answered as a child before life's experiences distorted your perception of yourself. Such a review of the words you selected will frequently transfer enough of them to another column to clearly define your correct and natural birth personality.

Combination of Four

When your profile scores are fairly even across, there are two possibilites. *One*, you really don't know yourself and probably don't care; or you are phlegmatic, it doesn't matter, and you have trouble making choices. Or, *two*, you are "double masked." The way you perceive yourself has been so distorted by life's experiences that you really don't know who you are. Refer to the Causes of Masking to see if any apply to you.

Remember, it takes a great deal of energy to wear a mask and live in a personality role that is not naturally yours. Our goal should be to take off the mask and live life to the fullest for which God created us.

Resources for Further Study

1. To Understand Personality Strengths and Weak-nesses: *Personality Plus*, Florence Littauer, Fleming H. Revell Co.
2. To Understand Masking: *Your Personality Tree*, Florence Littauer, Word Books.
3. To Understand Effects of Childhood Trauma: *Freeing Your Mind from Memories that Bind*, Fred & Florence Littauer, and *The Promise of Restoration*, Fred Littauer, Thomas Nelson Publishers.
4. To Understand Children's Personalities: *Raising Christians, Not Just Children*, Florence Littauer, Word Books.
5. To Understand Your Leadership Potential: *Personal-*

ities in Power, Florence Littauer, Huntington House.
6. To Understand Personalities in the Workplace: *Personality Puzzle*, Florence Littauer & Marita Littauer, Fleming H. Revell Co.

These invaluable books are available at your Christian bookstore.

3

How Can I Work Through My Anger?

—Annie Chapman

NO ONE HAS SEEN the wrath of Annie Chapman like the people who work at the many airports my family and I travel through each year. Something about being at the mercy of slow ticket agents, delayed flights, and strict carry-on baggage rules brings out the worst in me.

Just as we were heading for the airport after a concert recently, some appreciative concert-goers gave us an exquisite handmade mirror with a figure of Jesus as the Good Shepherd etched on the glass. Unfortunately, the mirror was too large for carry-on and wasn't packaged for the baggage compartment.

At the airport, I put on my sweetest smile and asked the gate agent if someone could hand-load the mirror into the baggage compartment rather than send it on the conveyor belt where it would face certain destruction. For all my niceness, I was told, "Look, lady, that's impossible."

As calmly as I could, I restated my dilemma, emphatically adding that we had invested untold dollars into this airline each week. Surely there was something the agent could do to help such loyal customers. My request was met with yet another cold reply.

Just as I was ready to leap over the counter, a male agent came over and interjected some gruff words in defense of his co-worker. I completely lost whatever composure I pretended to possess and quickly told my husband how uncooperative and rude the agents had been. Irritated that they had upset me, Steve went over and started writing down names and asking for the supervisor. Just then the female gate agent excitedly blurted out a plan. "I know what we can do!" she exclaimed. "Someone could walk the mirror into the baggage department and place it on top so it doesn't break."

My blood was boiling, not only because this woman had turned my original request into an exasperating conflict and then taken credit for resolving the issue, but because I feared someone might ask us what we did for a living. After the way we behaved, I was ashamed to admit we were Christians.

Granted, the squeaky wheel usually does get the grease, but now, every time I see the compassionate picture of Jesus on that mirror, I feel ashamed at the ungodly way I let my anger control my actions at the airport that day. How and when do we as Christians express our anger without crossing over the line to sin?

What Makes God Mad?

Anger is a legitimate emotion. God feels it, Jesus did, and so do we. The most commonly quoted verse in Scripture concerning anger is Ephesians 4:26: "In your anger do not sin." Biblically speaking, it's not sinful to feel anger. However, Scripture does warn us against sinning when we're mad. To get a handle on anger, it helps to look at Scripture for guidelines on legitimate causes and appropriate responses to anger.

First, anger is permissible when it stems from witnessing disobedience. Throughout the Bible we see that

God's wrath arose wherever wickedness abounded. Romans 1:18 warns, "The wrath of God is being revealed from heaven against all the godlessness and wickedness of men who suppress the truth by their wickedness. . . ." The consequences of embracing wickedness is demonstrated in the destruction of Sodom and Gomorrah (Genesis 19). Their resultant doom has stood as a warning to cultures throughout the centuries.

Our God is an angry God, to be sure. But He doesn't fly off the handle over petty issues. No, when God gets mad it's with good reason—we are disobeying Him.

In the same way, Jesus reserved His anger for critical matters. In Mark 3:5, Jesus' anger flared at those who criticized Him for healing a man's shriveled hand on the Sabbath. As Mark reads, "He [Jesus] looked around at them in anger and, deeply distressed at their stubborn hearts, said to the man, 'Stretch out your hand.' "

Though His blood pressure was probably spiking and He may have had some choice words on His tongue, Jesus managed to restrain himself and calmly address the issue of healing on the Sabbath. Jesus' behavior reflects the teaching of Proverbs 15:1, which sums up much of Scripture's counsel on expressing anger: "A gentle answer turns away wrath, but a harsh word stirs up anger." Jesus, in all His wisdom, realized that yelling at the Pharisees or belittling them for their stupidity over the issue of healing on the Sabbath would have created enmity between them, not to mention making Him guilty of sin.

Second, anger is acceptable when it stems from righteous indignation. Sometimes I find myself trying to justify my short fuse by pointing out that Jesus lost His temper once in a while too. Didn't He lash out at the money changers and overturn tables in the temple because they were making His Father's house into a "den of robbers"?

GETTING TO THE ROOT

Anger is often a clue to a deep personal need that is not being met. In many cases it is appropriate to be angry—at injustice, falsehood, cruelty. Jesus showed anger at the greed and materialism in His Father's house. Ask God to show you the root of your anger. Reflect on it in your journal until you understand it better.

—Luci

Unfortunately, most of the things we get angry about could hardly be called righteous. We get angry because we stub our toe, get overlooked for a promotion, or tire of a child's whining. Jesus became angry when someone else was being hurt. When the Pharisees scoffed at Him for healing on the Sabbath, another man's physical well-being was at stake. When He rampaged the temple, the money changers were exploiting the poor people by overcharging them for their animal sacrifices. Christian psychologist Archibald Hart put it well when he said in *Feeling Free* (Revell), "If we could get angry only at the things that Jesus got angry at, we could make a wonderful world."

Anger, if properly motivated and vented, is an emotion that can prompt us to act in positive ways. When I would hear Faye Waddleton, the former director of Planned Parenthood, speak out on the constitutional right of women to slaughter innocent babies, the rage I felt made me cry out, "Jesus, this is wrong!" My anger was a convicting anger that prompted me to fight for the lives of unborn children.

Likewise, righteous anger is the kind that causes us to run to the aid of a woman being attacked in a park, or support the prosecution of a child molester. We are justified in acting on our anger when it is in defense of someone, even when that person might be ourselves.

Taking Control of Anger

Many of us don't realize the extent to which anger— that which is neither righteous nor derived from a critical concern—controls us. Yet anger isn't always easy to identify. Sure, sometimes anger rules our lives in obvious displays of temper. We yell at our husband or slam a door. When I scream at the kids, "If you want to live to see your next birthday, you'd better get those dishes out of the den," I am undeniably confronted with the sinful outworking of my anger.

But sometimes anger masks itself. For instance, we may vent our anger at work by subconsciously becoming inefficient or by taking an extra-long coffee break, thinking this will get back at our boss for denying our request for a raise. Or an angry person may become accident prone, forgetful, or have sexual problems with a spouse. So how can we uncover as well as deal with our anger?

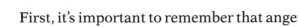

First, it's important to remember that anger, like happiness or any other emotion, is a choice. Yes, we may naturally feel the emotion, but it is up to us to decide whether we will give rise to it or deal with it productively and responsibly.

As I mentioned earlier, the airport tends to be my proving ground for how I handle anger. Just this past weekend the airline lost our luggage again so I was forced to buy a new pair of high heels for our concert. I was angry because I had a perfectly good pair in my suitcase. Although I was agitated by the situation, I took a minute to consciously say, "Okay, I don't have to get angry about this. I have a choice." Rather than let my anger control my thoughts and actions, I short-circuited the response and chose not to dwell on my anger.

Part of the reason anger brings out my aggressive nature is because I like to be in control. However, wanting to be in charge does not give me the right to chew people out when I get frustrated because things don't go as planned. In fact, recently when our flight was delayed, I was determined not to brood over the inconvenience and complain to the airline agents, but instead to use the time constructively. The experience inspired me to write a short article on how to use interruptions—life's speed bumps—as an opportunity.

Because our lives are clouded and warped by our old sinful nature, we need to fight the natural tendency to give in to anger and let it control us. Granted, blessing those who curse us is not the all-American game plan, but, as Christians, this is the choice we must continually make.

Second, when I feel myself starting to get out of control I need to curb my behavior by making sure I'm at my best physically. Have I established some positive habits, like a proper diet, sufficient sleep, and regular exercise? I know when I'm going full throttle on low fuel and little rest, I cannot meet the demands of my life in a godly way. Women, especially, sometimes harbor deep resentment for feeling overworked and under-appreciated. Steve says when I feel overworked it can be expensive. It's true. I will often overspend or buy something I've put off purchasing when I feel tired and angry. For me, tired and angry often goes hand in hand.

Too often, though, we let these feelings build until they explode in a fit of rage. Sure, by the time I scream,

"I am not the house slave," my family willingly jumps up and pitches in. But it's unhealthy and sinful to act out of rage.

———— ∞ ————

Third, I often need to take a few minutes to sort out why my temper is flaring up, in order to dissipate my anger. I've learned to ask myself some important questions when I get angry. *What will my anger change or accomplish? What in particular is causing the anger? Am I tired, hungry, disappointed? Is my anger the result of my own mistakes?*

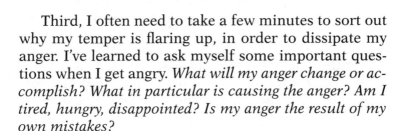

WORK IT THROUGH

To handle anger, first face the fact that you are angry. So often I rationalize that good Christians are never angry, therefore I must deny my emotions so I can tell myself I'm a spiritually mature Christian. Second, accept the fact you will occasionally get angry. Finally, sit down and list everything that you are mad about. It may be a long list! Once it is on paper, you will see the source of your anger and be able to work through the list. Take some time each day to prayerfully ask the Lord, "Does this need forgiveness, acceptance, or action?" The Lord will direct your path and provide relief.

—Florence

Then I offer my thoughts—as negative as they may be—to the Lord. The experience can become an opportunity to grow and mature in your Christian walk. Second Corinthians 12:9–10 affirms this truth, "Therefore I will boast all the more gladly about my weaknesses, so that Christ's power may rest on me. That is why, for

Christ's sake, I delight in weakness, in insults, in hardships, in persecutions, in difficulties. For when I am weak, then I am strong." Admitting my weakness in the area of anger is the beginning of allowing Christ's strength to fortify me and continue to change me. My weakness actually becomes a container for His strength.

Fourth, our desires, demands, and expectations also play into how well we handle our anger. When I'm working to meet a deadline and enter the kitchen only to see a sink full of dirty dishes, I'm not going to be very receptive to the woman who calls asking for my help with the band boosters. Now, if I have a few minutes to get my bearings and regain some control, I can usually ride out the storm. The kids have learned to read my signs. They know when I nervously run my fingers through my hair and have a frown across my face, it's time to go outside and find something to do.

Finally, it's helpful to become aware of the circumstances that feed into an angry mood. For instance, background noise, like the TV or radio, grate on my nerves and make me irritable when I'm trying to concentrate or talk with the kids. I've learned to turn off all the extraneous noise, and the resulting calm is amazing.

Avoiding irritating or disruptive situations is another way to get a handle on your anger. I get keyed up reading about social issues like abortion and pornography. Over time, I have learned not to read news on these subjects before I go to bed. This way I get a better night of sleep and approach the issues more rationally the next morning.

Prescription for Peace

For some of us, anger is not a significant issue. We may feel it, but it isn't a gateway to sin. For others, though, anger is a powerful temptation to be reckoned with. Before I was a Christian, I would sin in my anger and not think anything of it. If someone said something I didn't like, I would just as soon slap him than deal with my emotions constructively. I thought I would feel better if I could physically vent my feelings, but there was always room in my heart for more anger to replace whatever was just released.

Thankfully, I now have the ultimate role model in Jesus Christ, and as I have gradually given over different areas of my life, including the way I handle anger, He has helped transform my heart and mind to understand and work on the way I deal with my temper.

Entertaining negative thoughts, fostering hurt feelings, or nursing grudges—these are the habits that pollute our life with sin. As Christians, we're not immune to the effects of anger, but we do have a Savior whose strength is perfected in our weakness. We only need to ask and He will send His Spirit to replace our anger with peace.

Make It Happen

1. Take some time to consider the situations, people, or places that tend to breed anger in your heart. Try to become conscious of your response to anger. Do you let it control you or are you in control of it? Ask God for forgiveness for the times you have crossed over the line from merely feeling the emotion to acting in sin because of it.

2. Dip into Proverbs each day for some counsel on the effects of anger and how to handle it. Ask God to give you a soft answer to keep you from stirring up wrath in others.

3. Meditate on James 1:19–20: "Everyone should be quick to listen, slow to speak and slow to become angry, for man's anger does not bring about the righteous life that God desires." Begin to incorporate this instruction into your response to situations that make you angry.

71

Connecting Anger With Love
Kelsey Menehan

Most of us feel uneasy and confused—if not downright alarmed—about the emotion of anger. Given what we know about its destructive potential, it's little wonder we often bury our angry feelings. As women, we've been conditioned to be nurturers and peacemakers, so we often turn our anger inward.

Whether we tend to "blow up" or "clam up" probably depends on our background, our personality, and our religious training. But neither extreme allows for the kind of intimacy in relationships we so desperately want. Is there a better way, a middle ground where Christians can deal constructively with their anger in a way that can lead to greater intimacy?

Anger no longer has to be seen as an automatic threat to intimacy but as a possible pathway to greater intimacy. Instead of suppressing our anger out of fear, we can begin to connect in a deeper way with ourselves and others.

Well-known Christian counselor David Mace believes many marriages fail because the partners are unable to deal creatively with their anger. His insights apply to any close relationship. Mace believes there is a better way for those with the courage and tenacity to try it. He boils it down to three steps:

1. Recognize that anger is a healthy emotion and not necessarily sinful. It is as legitimate to say to a friend or loved one, "I am angry," as it is to say, "I am hungry" or "I am sad." When you know you are angry, communicate this as soon as possible.

2. Make a conscious choice not to vent your anger or attack the other person. Don't put your partner on the defensive, but

72

instead allow him or her to develop a compassionate concern toward you as well as communicate a desire to understand how and why the anger arose.

3. Recognize that unresolved anger can be a barrier to intimacy and accept equal responsibility for clearing it up. Together, carefully examine the angry situation to discover the roots of the strong feelings.

Our anger can be a tremendous gift, if we dare to look at the feelings it covers up. Christian psychologist Larry Crabb believes we can never grow as Christians until we face the realities of our own internal fears. "Christ wants us to face reality as it is, including all the fears, hurts, resentments, and self-protective motives we work hard to keep out of sight, and to emerge as changed people," he writes in *Inside Out* (NavPress). "Not pretenders. Not perfect. But more able to deeply love because we're more aware of His love."

Learning to recognize our strong feelings and to direct them in positive ways is not an easy process. It takes practice, and we must allow ourselves and those we love room to fail. But it is worth the effort. Careening between the extremes of venting or suppressing our anger almost certainly cuts us off from the very things we desire: more intimate, authentic relationships with others, and especially with God.

—From *Today's Christian Woman* (March/April 1991)

4

Should I Trust My Feelings of Love?

—*Luci Shaw*

ANYONE WHO HAS BEEN married for more than a week can attest to the fact that the "feelings" we associate with love do in fact shift and change—at least on occasion. The sweaty palms, racing heart, euphoria, and the inability to concentrate—those intense feelings many of us associate with falling in love—don't last forever.

Still, many of us expect our romantic feelings of love to continue. When they don't, we feel disillusioned about love—not to mention our partner. As the feelings fade, secret questions like, "Is this all there is?" or "Does it mean I no longer love my spouse?" fill the cracks of our hearts where romance once lived.

But before you resign yourself to a relationship devoid of sentiment or excitement, remember that the ebb and flow of these intense feelings is normal. And, most important, realize that our feelings do not comprise the essence, or the foundation, of love.

Love Redefined

Often when we think about love, we view ourselves as swept away by romance, overwhelmed by our feelings. When the feelings we associate with love fade, we need to remember that God created us with the rational capacity to see love as a choice apart from pure emotion.

A LITTLE GOES A LONG WAY

Don't confuse love with passion. Passion is a euphoric state that takes your breath away, but it isn't practical to live the next forty years of your married life continually in that state. Steve and I have been married twenty years and the passion is still there and wonderful, but I liken it to Thanksgiving dinner—the meal is fabulous, but you wouldn't want it every day.

—Annie

Studying the character of God the Father helps me to understand the rational side of love. It was our heavenly Father's will that brought Him into a loving relationship with us. Filled with sin, we were anything but lovable. In Deuteronomy God tells the Israelites He loves them simply because He *chooses* to love them. Likewise, His love for us is based on a choice He has already made—a choice not based on our goodness, faithfulness, or obedience. God persists in His love "just because."

When I met my second husband, John, I respected and instinctively trusted him. However, thinking of him in a romantic sense was not an automatic response. I had to choose for our relationship to grow in that direction. Don't get me wrong, I value the emotional component of love. But I also know, having lived for a while, that when we put too much stock in the romantic feelings of love, we can discount our personal will and decision-making ability regarding love. We begin to view love as something beyond our control, when in reality it is a choice—a doorway through which we choose to move.

Besides being a choice, love also involves commitment to that choice. In the past two years, since I remarried and moved from Chicago to California, I have had to adapt to a new culture as well as my new family—John and his two college-age children, a son and a daughter.

I knew from the beginning I wanted a loving relationship with my stepchildren. I also knew that such a relationship would not be automatic. I needed the will to love these young strangers, and likewise they needed the will to love me. It's only through intentionally choosing to act lovingly and getting to know them personally that the feelings of love can come and be reciprocated. This isn't easy or automatic. There are multiple roadblocks on both sides.

Since we were all committed to working toward a loving relationship, after many ups and downs, I was able to write in my journal, "We have reached a place where we do care about each other. We know how important a good working, loving relationship can be."

Commitment is also integral in a marriage; it helps us keep going when our feelings of love might waver. I know at times I get really irritated with John (and he with me). And, I'll admit, were it not for our vows to remain steadfast in our commitment to each other and to honor God through our marriage, we might be tempted to throw in the towel. Without commitment, love—true love—doesn't stand a chance of maturing and growing. Our feelings of love will ebb and flow, but what keeps love afloat during the changing tides is commitment, patience, and determination.

I'M COMMITTED TO YOU

Commitment makes all the difference. Fred and I are committed to one another. With that as a foundation of our love, the question, "Do I still love him or don't I?" is a moot point.
—Florence

Where does the strength to make the choice to love and follow through on our commitment come from? Should we act as if we love someone when our feelings seem to tell us otherwise? How do we meet the needs of the one we love when we might not feel lovingly toward that person?

For me, the answer to these questions didn't come until after nearly thirty years of marriage to my first husband, Harold. The entire time we were married, I had a deep longing to know that God was real and that He cared about me personally. For all of his best efforts to meet my needs, Harold could not fill this spiritual void for me. It took some years of widowhood, after his death from cancer, to grow my own spiritual muscles. I am a questioner, a natural skeptic, not satisfied with superficial answers. Though others can give me wisdom and support, I need to develop the direct, personal friendship with God that will allow me to go through dark, turbulent trials without letting go of Him. Sometimes He teaches us through silence. Often God was "dark" to me, as I described in *God in the Dark* (Zondervan). During such times I've learned that faith isn't an easy belief but the patience to wait—to let God be God—to learn the lessons that are taught only through God's absence. I call such times the "winter of the heart," when I lie in wait for spring and sunshine and the green growth it produces. This is God's supremely creative act—to know when and how to show himself to me. I am a poet, a creator, and just as my poems take months and years to mature, I know that I am growing in God's image, in His time, under His creative providence. That is the patience of faith.

Once I found my significance in my Creator I was able to give redemptively to others even when I didn't feel like it. By learning to trust in God's ever-fixed (though not always felt) love for me, I could love others, regardless of my feelings. Unless we are giving out of the reservoir of love we have for and from God, we can't possibly meet the needs of those we love.

My long-term personal and professional relationship with a well-known woman author was dramatically enhanced recently. She had been badly injured in an auto accident far from home, and, obeying an impulse that I recognized to be from God, I flew to be with her for several days in a distant hospital. It evidently meant a great deal to her that I would show that kind of loving commitment. I had long revered and admired her, but I felt a new kind of love and closeness when I witnessed her great pain and weakness and her gratefulness that I had taken time out of a busy schedule to care for her. We spent much time reading Scripture, and praying together, baring our souls, telling stories, engaging in "God talk and book talk," and our hearts were united in a deeper way than ever before. Now we are writing a book together on friendship!

Tracking the Tide

Most of us expect life to move along on an even keel, but in reality—and especially in our relationships— things seldom flow smoothly. Because we operate under the assumption that they should, often we're not prepared to deal with the disappointment that comes when our feelings ebb and flow.

To best handle the inevitable ups and downs of relationships and our feelings about them, I've found it helpful to keep a journal. For me, journaling is a form of prayer. I use my journal to express my responses to God, my needs, my concerns, and my feelings (or lack of feelings). Basically, it's a way for me to think my thoughts in the presence of God, and it's been an invaluable way to recognize how God has made himself known to me during the down cycles of my life.

As I have adjusted to life in California and sorted out my relationship with John and his children, my journal has continued to be my confidante. It helps me track the events and feelings I had and continue to have as we work toward mutual respect and love for one another. As I look back through the pages, I can see the shifts in my emotions—how my feelings changed from week to week about these new relationships. I could see where progress in the relationships was made, what the problems were, and how problems might be overcome. If I hadn't spent the time working my thoughts out in my journal and with God, I think I would have felt much more desperate about wanting a loving relationship with my new family yet not always feeling that love.

Journaling may not be for everyone, but it is a useful tool for tracking the growth of your relationships with others and with God. Then, when you hit dry spots that leave you feeling disillusioned and uncertain, you've got your own record of life, and you can review how you've moved beyond these desert experiences in the past.

Time and experience are often the best teachers as we adjust to the changing tides of our feelings of love. After thirty-three years of lessons on love and commitment in my first marriage, I believe I have a good understanding of what my new marriage should entail. I now know that love involves choice and commitment. Love is not only feelings. We may not always feel love, but if we make a choice to love and follow that with a commitment to love and honesty, with time the feelings will follow. Even then, we can expect our feelings of love to ebb and flow. And for that reason feelings cannot serve as the only benchmark to measure the quality of my relationships but, instead, my actions of love—my concern and my willingness to meet another's needs.

Make It Happen

1. Begin to keep a journal of your feelings about the relationships in your life, including your relationship with God. As you review what you have written, note any trends or patterns in the way your feelings seem to ebb and flow. Try to write one "feeling" statement and one "thinking" statement about yourself every day!

2. Look up several references about love in your Bible's concordance. Memorize one that speaks directly to you about loving others unconditionally, and repeat it silently to yourself whenever your feelings prompt you to withhold love or doubt another's love for you.

3. To keep love from becoming an emotional roller-coaster, learn to focus on the needs of those you love and how you can meet those needs rather than on how you "feel" about the person. Remember, feelings change quickly and often aren't based on more than the here and now.

When You've Lost That Lovin' Feeling
Jan Johnson

"I don't feel as if I love you anymore," I blurted out one evening to my spouse. For the first time my feelings for my husband of one year had languished. I felt devastated. I kept thinking, *This couldn't happen to us—we're Christians.*

Now, after fifteen years of ups and downs, those hollow feelings don't surprise me. I've learned these empty feelings are normal. What I do with them makes all the difference. If I view them as bad, they discourage me, but if I view them as a normal growing stage, they spawn a more mature marriage.

As unromantic and unspontaneous as it sounds, my husband, Greg, and I find we have to work at creating those tender, romantic feelings. And we've found that consistently working on our marriage decreases the frequency of the dry spells. Here are a few of our strategies:

Pray Together

I felt disgusted with Greg when a career change left him unemployed and doing odd jobs for a year. It seemed no job was good enough for him.

Then we prayed together about it. I listened to his prayer and realized the desperation he felt in finding the "right" job. The prayer helped me, not because it changed our circumstance, but because it changed my perspective. I felt tender and caring for Greg again.

Observe Your Spouse's Personal Growth

My friend Wanda says that seeing her husband mature re-generates her tender feelings. "I've prayed that Bill will become the man God wants him to be and I can see it happening. As he becomes more confident and controlled, I'm more attracted to him." We pray for God to change our husbands and then forget to notice His handiwork. Greg now handles money better, he understands our children better, and he puts my desires ahead of his more often. Such observations spark tenderness within me.

Talk About the Blahs

As our communication skills have sharpened, Greg and I are better able to talk about those times our marriage lacks warmth. Now, instead of accusatory outbursts, I offer calm diagnoses of a dilemma I'm sure we can work out as a team. Sometimes I find that he's feeling the same way, and we feel an odd camaraderie in our determination to work on it.

Act "As If"

The most helpful strategy I've found is to act as if I do feel those warm feelings even when I don't. In his video series, "Counseling by Encouragement," Dr. Larry Crabb calls this being "a hypocrite to your feelings." It works. After "pretending" to feel enamored with my husband, those romantic feelings come back. This may sound phony, but following my feelings doesn't work—they swell and subside without warning. By aligning my feelings with my commitment to my husband, I'm taking "captive every thought to make it obedient to Christ" (2 Corinthians 10:5). If I act in faith, I will have those feelings tomorrow.

—Adapted from *Today's Christian Woman* (September/October 1989)

PART TWO

FOR WOMEN ONLY

HARD AS WE MAY TRY, there are some facets of our makeup as women that men may never fully comprehend. Questions like, "Why do I have such a strong emotional attachment to my home?" or "How do I keep PMS from ruling my emotions?" probe at the heart of what it means to be uniquely female.

As Annie discusses the challenges of PMS in this section, she cites Proverbs 14:1: "The wise woman builds her house, but with her own hands the foolish one tears hers down." While Annie applies this verse to the specific problems of PMS, it also relates to our need to express our other emotions in a healthy manner so we don't run the risk of destroying our own households.

In the following chapters, Annie, Florence, and Luci offer their advice and encouragement on how to get through the month without being dominated by your hormones, how to share your deepest feelings with your partner in a way he can understand, and, above all, how to keep on top of your emotions so you are ever building your relationships.

5

Why Am I So Emotionally Attached to My Home?

—*Luci Shaw*

THREE YEARS AGO I packed up more than thirty years' worth of memories and belongings from my midwestern home and transported everything to California to start a new life with John. The move was an emotional experience, to say the least. I was exhilarated and challenged by the adventure of a new life, a new environment, but I was also feeling depressed at the uprooting and the loss of the familiar and valued elements after living in Illinois for more than forty years. In a sense, I felt as though I were leaving everything behind. The identity and feeling of rootedness I had worked so hard to achieve all those years was gone, and now I was starting from scratch as I worked to integrate my things and my life into John's home.

My feelings of security and attachment I had in the Midwest started to return once I moved some of my belongings into my new home. I gained an even greater sense of rootedness and security when I was able to build on an office/library space, as an addition to John's house, that I could call my own. And as I began to feel more comfortable in my new surroundings, I started to reflect on the meaning of home and why it holds such a strong emotional tie for women.

A Glimpse of the Ultimate Home

It's fair to say that as women we naturally possess a rooting or nesting instinct that makes us want to create a place of security for our family as well as ourselves. We want to have a place of peace, privacy, and refuge. It's as if we want to build a place where community is possible. We need homes for security and protection from the elements just as our hearts need to find a spiritual home in God. Even my small dome tent, which I can erect in ten minutes, gives me a sense of security and a haven when I stop for the night at a state or national park when I'm driving across the country—a center for sleep and privacy as well as protection from wind and rain.

Perhaps God, in his infinite wisdom, created us with an almost universal desire to make a haven for our families, a center in a crazy world, to give us a foretaste of what it will feel like to live in the truest of all homes—heaven. We live in an increasingly mobile society. Transience is becoming a way of life. No longer do families grow up and stay in the town where their grandparents live. Rootlessness, both physical and spiritual, characterizes most Americans today. That, and the knowledge of our own impermanence, our mortality, fills us with a desire for centeredness in God.

Apart from the spiritual reasons we are wired for rootedness, our homes often fulfill deep emotional and psychological needs for us. A few years ago, my son-in-law built a home for me in Bellingham, Washington. It's a place of safety, seclusion, and possibility for me, with its wood stove and skylights, surrounded by the green forest and the hush of the stream that flows below the outside deck—an anchor in times of stress. As I worked with him on designing this house, I realized that a home, especially for a woman, is an extension of herself. And as a result, on an emotional level, I wanted my home to represent my best qualities and my truest values. In a sense, creating a home is like creating a work of art.

With my home in Bellingham I tried to make it as functional as possible, but I also wanted it to be beautiful—something that would represent me so when friends came to my home they would see evidence of my taste, creativity, or organizational ability. My desire for my home to look "just right" wasn't based on my wanting it to look better than someone else's home; instead, subconsciously I realized that my home was *a reflection of me.*

A word of caution about our homes, though. While it is perfectly normal and legitimate to want to create a home that reflects our individual taste and personality, we need to take care that our self-image doesn't become too wrapped up in a physical structure and our home doesn't become our idol.

ANY ROOF WILL DO

Because I grew up living in three tiny rooms behind my father's store, I longed for a real house with a front door that opened onto something besides a store. I'm sure my emotional need for a house surpassed the average woman's desire for a home. As I have matured in my spiritual growth, I have finally come to a point where I can honestly say, "I would live happily in a motel." In fact, with almost 300 days a year on the road, I do!

—Florence

Down the street from where John and I live is an immense, three-story, seven-bedroom home. A couple lives in this huge house and, while they have no children nor do they seem to entertain, they continue to pour money into the house. Granted, I don't know what their lives consist of, but from outward appearances it seems that they don't know what else to do with their lives or their money other than improve their home. Expensive and luxurious as it is, their house seems empty and cold—a fortress that excludes rather than a home that welcomes.

A second caution about our homes is that we don't want to let them take priority over the relationships in our lives. I've known of women who spend so much time trying to create the picture-perfect home that their families end up feeling neglected. My own mother, an immaculate housekeeper, was so worried about fingerprints on the woodwork and dirt tracked into the house, that she never could relax and enjoy her grandchildren when we came to visit her, and they never felt at home with her.

Open Door Policy

Since we are so instinctively driven to create a sense of rootedness, we need to occasionally look at our priorities for our home. As Christians, I believe a top priority should be to create a home that makes it possible for people to come together—both family and friends. When we view our home in this light—as a focal point for welcome and outreach—our homes take their proper place among the many other priorities in our lives. As I look at that big, cold house down the street from us I can't help but feel a sense of sadness. With no family, and little entertaining, the house is just an idol—a shell that isn't used for the benefit of anyone but the owners.

Our house is used as a way-station for traveling

friends and family members, and also as a regular meeting place for Bible studies, prayer and journaling support groups, Christian artists, and foreign students.

Paradoxically, we often feel most fulfilled and satisfied when we give. Having guests for an evening (or a week) expresses that part of us that longs to be like God, who reaches out and enfolds others in love.

HOME SWEET HOME

Steve and I spend a fair amount of time traveling. One night, as the children and I were about to drift off to sleep in our hotel room, Steve said, "I wonder who slobbered on this pillow last night?"

"Yuck," the children squealed. My sentiments exactly. To come home to our clean beds, or even our own messy laundry room, is a blessing I never take for granted. Home to me is our safe place. Inside the walls of our house everyone knows they are free to be themselves without the fear of rejection. Each person knows they will be loved for themselves. Not every home offers emotional security, but each should.

—Annie

A second priority for our homes, beyond nurturing relationships, is efficient operation. Most women can't live in chaos. One prevailing theme in my life is to bring order out of chaos—both in my writing and in my life. I remember when I moved into John's house, there was set after set of measuring cups and several electric mixers! Apparently, whenever a set of measuring cups couldn't be found, another was purchased. I found this irritating at first, but I laugh about it now that some order has been brought to the kitchen.

As we work to bring order to our homes, the reward is that they become launching pads for ourselves and the rest of our family. If your home is organized, it can empower you to do a great deal more in life—to reach out beyond your home to the needs of others. I know that when my garden flowers are flourishing, my floors are swept, and my desk is organized, I feel much freer to show hospitality.

Take Time to Talk

In general, a woman can't live without some sort of center in her life and most often that center is her home. I believe that men, on the other hand, might hop into a plane and move from place to place around the country without a sense of loss at each juncture. With such different needs and perspectives often it's hard for a man to understand just why a woman's home is so centrally important to her.

I know when I moved to California it took John some time to understand the emotional upheaval I was experiencing because I had lost my sense of rootedness. What helped him see my perspective is that I took time to explain to him how I felt and why. I told him, "John, when pictures of my children are on the wall, and I can put an oriental rug in the living room and my books in bookcases, I know this isn't just your house, but *our* home." Fortunately, John, being the perceptive person he is, began to see things from my point of view, but that wouldn't have happened had I kept quiet.

In the process of combining our two homes into one, John has shown me that in many ways men do have an emotional attachment to their homes, but they express it differently. For instance, while my concern is for the wallpaper or curtains, John's may be for a door that isn't hung properly or a fixture that needs repairing. By valuing each other's particular areas of strength and interest, John and I have been able to create a home that is truly ours.

While we as women experience a more intense emotional attachment to our homes, and for us it represents who we are and the security we desire, we need to remember that in the end it serves as an unfinished model of the perfect dwelling place—our home with God.

Make It Happen

1. How pleased are you with your home? Is getting it "just right" becoming an obsession? Ask God for balance in your perspective regarding how much time and energy you should spend on your home.

2. Is your home a haven? Does your family look forward to coming home at the end of the day? Does it serve as a "launching pad?" Together with your family discuss ways that your home can become a nurturing, positive place that will strengthen each family member for the challenges he or she faces outside the home.

3. Think through the concept of home as a tool for outreach. Consider ways to maximize the space and comfort of your home to serve others. Perhaps you could host a regular Bible study or invite foreign exchange students to stay with you. Prayerfully open yourself up to possible ministry opportunities in your home.

6

How Can I Keep PMS From Ruling My Emotions?

—Annie Chapman

THE WAY I FIGURE IT, I'm sane one week a month. The week before my period is terrible. I'm bloated, and bloating is definitely a female thing. Have you ever heard a man complain, "My pants sure are tight today. I must be bloated"? Besides not being able to wear certain clothes during this time, I'm also hateful. The worst part, however, is the cravings. I'm like a ravenous wolf. I could eat a mule down to the hoof. There's no denying it, the whole week before my period is shot.

Then there's the week of. On top of feeling miserable and bloated, my varicose veins hurt so bad I can barely walk. I can't jog or swim at the YMCA. It's a lousy time of the month.

Then there's the week after my period. I spend seven full days making amends for all the terrible things I've done and said the two weeks before. All totaled, that's only twelve weeks of sanity a year!

I once heard on a television news show of a judge who let a woman who had murdered her husband go free. The reason: The judge believed her period had led her to commit such a heinous crime. Though few of us would admit that our period, or the symptoms that proceed it (premenstrual syndrome or **PMS**) would cause us to kill, most of us would concede that we tend to do things out of character because of our monthly cycle. And while few women are as emotionally unbalanced from **PMS** as the woman who murdered her husband, for most of us **PMS** remains a bothersome, disruptive part of our life. The good news is many of us can learn effective ways to deal with **PMS** and minimize its effects on our emotions and the lives of others.

Know Yourself

Scripture says, "The wise woman builds her house, but with her own hands the foolish one tears hers down" (Proverbs 14:1). It's a foolish woman who is affected by **PMS** in such a way that it disrupts her relationships, and yet doesn't take steps to understand it and guard against it. We may be miserable, but we don't need to punish those we love for something they can't help.

LOOK TO YOUR PAST

As I talk with women, I find that many with extreme symptoms of PMS were sexually interfered with as children and have buried the incident. When the source is uncovered through prayer, the symptoms of PMS lessen and often disappear completely.

—Florence

Thankfully, there are ways to improve the ratio of bad weeks to good. If you think you suffer from **PMS**, try tracking your daily habits and symptoms on a calendar. First, track your daily emotional health. Make a note of the times you cry easily, feel irritable or negative about life, or seem to have a short fuse. Second, keep track of any physical symptoms you experience like backaches, bloating, or cramping.

Medical experts recommend keeping an accurate log for three months to be sure that symptoms like bloating or cramps are truly premenstrual—those that occur during the two weeks between ovulation and your period. If the symptoms don't fit within this time frame, then it's wise to make an appointment with your physician for further studies.

Once you have an understanding of the effects your hormones have on your life, and patterns begin to emerge, try to plan ahead for the coming month to compensate for those days when you likely will be unable to respond to people and responsibilities in a positive way. Agree with your spouse not to discuss volatile issues the week before your period, as my friend learned to do. Once she discovered that her worst arguments with her husband always occurred two to three days before her period, she took steps to avoid major confrontations during this time. Similarly, it's wise to hold off on planning your family budget and forego inviting out-of-town guests for an overnight stay.

I always assume I'll remember which days I get cranky or have uncontrollable cravings and, as a result, often fail to keep track of my cycle. Consequently, when PMS strikes and I'm close to losing my sanity, I end up feeling as though the cause for my behavior is some gross sin in my life rather than recognizing it as a bad case of PMS. When I get my period a few days later, I realize it wasn't that I had fallen away from the Lord, but that my hormones were doing jumping jacks in my brain.

Thankfully, even though I often fail to keep a record of my daily habits and responses to the world, I found out a while ago that Steve keeps track of my cycle. He watches for the signs of stress and fatigue and knows when **PMS** is in full force. In fact, I'll say, "I don't know what's wrong with me today," and Steve will say, "Well, it's about time for your period."

Fortunately, Steve's a wise man, and when he knows I'm battling **PMS**, he often takes the kids out to dinner instead of having me cook. I can join them if I want, but sometimes I choose to enjoy a few hours to myself.

DON'T LEAVE HIM IN THE DARK

A woman's menstrual cycle has an immense effect on her emotional responses. And like the ebb and flow of relationships, there is also an ebb and flow to a woman's hormones that she must deal with. A significant part of dealing with PMS is helping your husband understand what is happening to you each month and realize how greatly it can affect you emotionally.

—Luci

While it helps to plan your life around **PMS**, obviously there are many variables you simply cannot determine ahead of time. For those times you simply need to pray for an extra dose of grace. Ask God to support you through this difficult time, and cut yourself some slack. A friend of mine knows she always gets extra critical of her looks before her period. Knowing that, she tries to withhold any judgment until after her period is over. If she still hates her hairstyle after her period has passed, then she gets it cut. But she's learned not to make any rash decisions about her looks until she's past her premenstrual stage.

Take Control

PMS is now more widely accepted as a true medical condition, and physicians, on occasion, do recommend medical treatment for those suffering from severe symptoms. While many of these treatments are effective in combating the annoying symptoms of PMS, there are also a range of self-help remedies that typically help most PMS sufferers. For instance, rather than use an over-the-counter or prescription diuretic to limit the bloating, I have found that adding lemon to my water and eating fruits like strawberries and grapefruit help reduce my symptoms. I also try to lower my salt intake.

Medical experts also recommend eliminating—or at least reducing—your caffeine, sugar, and alcohol consumption seven to ten days before your period. In a recent study, it was found that the symptoms of PMS were 30 percent higher in women who drank one caffeinated beverage per day. As you eliminate caffeine from your diet, taper off gradually to avoid headaches and other side-effects that accompany caffeine withdrawal.

I try to eat three meals and three nutritious snacks a day to ward off my tendency to binge the days before my period. Eating healthy food at regular intervals helps my blood sugar stay on a more even keel, and I'm less tempted to binge on fatty, sugary snacks.

Another self-help remedy for PMS is exercise—if possible, thirty minutes a day. Now I'll admit, exercise is a real challenge for me. But when I am successful in maintaining a regular exercise program, I am much more able to cope with PMS. So even though I don't enjoy the discipline exercise requires of me, the payback of keeping PMS under control is worth the cost.

No Excuses

Anyone who suffers from PMS, as I do, knows what it's like to lose it emotionally. We blow up and launch into an angry tirade aimed at our husbands, children, co-workers, or friends. We weep easily and think mean thoughts. We question our emotional stability. Our behavior is normal, and because we lose it on occasion doesn't mean we're bad Christians. Yet, while it helps to realize that our out-of-whack feelings are not an emotional problem but a chemical one, we have to be careful not to use **PMS** as an excuse for sinful behavior. Too many times I have rationalized my sin by saying, "I have **PMS**." The fact is, if I say or do hurtful things out of anger, whether it's because my hormones have gone bonkers or not, my actions are still sin. I may not have wonderful thoughts toward my family while I'm in the throes of my cycle, but I still have a choice whether to speak my mind or stay silent. Gradually, I'm realizing the wisdom of biting my tongue and waiting for my positive perspective to return.

There are still times when I let **PMS** get the best of me and say things I shouldn't. When this happens, I am quick to apologize and not make excuses for my behavior. I just say, "I'm sorry. Mom doesn't mean to be nasty to you. I need your prayers especially this week."

My daughter Heidi has started her periods. Because this is such an important milestone in a girl's life, I want her to feel good about the changes taking place in her body. Yet I wonder if my negativity about getting my period every month has tainted her outlook. Instead of viewing my cycle as God's creative way, I tend to see it as an inconvenience. We're programmed to think our periods are horrible rather than a wonderful, God-given process in our bodies.

Heidi came home the other day with the exciting news that her friend had "started." They even threw a party for her. Maybe, if I can continue to hold my tongue and keep from complaining about my throbbing varicose veins, Heidi will have a better shot at appreciating what is taking place in her body every month.

With a daughter who is fast approaching womanhood, I've had a chance to view my menstrual cycle in a different light. Watching Heidi go through this experience has reminded me that the uncomfortable symptoms and hassles we go through every month are part of an amazing process. We truly are fearfully and wonderfully made. Unfortunately, 'round about the time I've got a handle on all of this, I'll be ready to enter menopause!

Make It Happen

1. Control your level of stress by not overloading your schedule. Draw a line through your PMS week on the calendar so you'll remember to limit your interaction with others to only those essential contacts and responsibilities.

2. Keep up with your daily devotions, even if your emotional swings from PMS make you want to do otherwise. It's tempting to let our time with God be dictated by hormonal swings, but often what we end up doing is cutting out the strength and support available from God just when we need it most.

3. Recognize that life goes in cycles. There may be times when you're full of energy and in a positive mood, and other times you're not. Enjoy life to the fullest when you're on top of the world. Give yourself a break and use the time when you're low as an opportunity to reflect and regroup.

7

How Can I Explain My Emotions to My Husband?

—Florence Littauer

FRED AND I HAVE BEEN MARRIED more than forty years. We travel everywhere together, we're with one another around the clock, and we actually have fun. This hasn't always been the case.

Sixteen years into our marriage, we were both discouraged. In today's world we would have probably divorced, but we had a sense of commitment that kept us together. Neither Fred nor I had ever taken the time to develop listening skills or understand each other's unique personality. So, when we endured the excruciating loss of two brain-damaged sons, these weak spots nearly caused our marriage to give out.

There were no books, tapes, or seminars on grief or marriage at the time and, because neither of us was a good listener, we were unable to tend to the other's grief, much less address any of the ongoing issues in our marriage. Privately, we each resolved to stay married for the sake of our two daughters. The reality was that neither Fred nor I had bonded with each other emotionally, so we grew further and further apart as we tried to cope with the many difficult issues that faced us as parents of children with severe disabilities.

Whenever I tried to discuss my feelings about the dilemmas we faced, Fred would offer point by point solutions to each problem. He gave me quick answers to everything, but I didn't want answers. What I wanted was someone to listen to me without judging me or making me feel stupid. I wondered, "Is it too much to ask him to listen to me and take my feelings seriously?" Fred couldn't understand why anyone would want to waste time discussing a problem without coming up with an immediate solution. I, in turn, viewed his answers as a lack of compassion and empathy—a sign that he didn't care about me or what I was feeling.

One day I asked Fred, "Wouldn't you rather be my friend instead of me having to talk to six other women about a problem I'm having?"

"Of course I want to be your friend," Fred replied.

"I like my friends a lot better than you because they listen. They don't give me answers," I said.

My comment stopped Fred in his tracks. He finally understood that his answers, rather than solving my problems, only forced me to go to other people for emotional intimacy. He realized then that maybe he had better stop giving me advice and start listening.

HE'S NO MIND READER

As a newlywed, I used to think, "If Steve really loved me he could read my mind." One day I finally realized how ridiculous I was being. No human being can read someone else's mind. I was expecting Steve to be God. From then on I would say to Steve, "Tell me you think I'm beautiful, I'm waiting. Tell me you think I'm smart. Tell me you love me." Though I would say it jokingly, I wanted him to understand what I needed from him emotionally, and with time he did.

—Annie

Are Men Naturally Bad Listeners?

Though Fred and I faced some uncommon crises that magnified the cracks in our relationship, many marriages suffer the same basic problem as ours—we did not take the time to listen to each other. With Fred so quick to zero in on the nuts and bolts of every issue, he never took the time to hear the feelings behind the facts, which, to my mind, were the essence of the events I tried to relate to him.

Research indicates that Fred's behavior is a typical male response. According to experts in gender studies, the way the male brain is formed predisposes men to operate on a more rational level. The female brain, on the other hand, develops in a way that allows us to more naturally filter thoughts and experiences through the lens of emotion. Where a man generally wants to take the shortest path to get from point A to point B, a woman doesn't mind taking a few side-trips along the way to make the process more interesting.

Granted, these gender differences don't apply to all men and women. But knowing that basic physiological differences do exist between men and women helps me see Fred's style of communicating in a new light. I began to understand that Fred isn't a bad listener. He just listens for different things than I do.

For instance, before I understood how Fred listened, if a water pipe broke and flooded our basement, I might have greeted him at the door in near hysterics, wanting to relate every awful detail of my horrendous day. I discovered, however, when I start to sound irrational, Fred tunes me out. He simply does not hear me.

Now, when I have something important to tell him, I try to deliver it first in outline form. "We have a serious problem. There's a leak in the basement. Would you call someone immediately to fix it." Within a few minutes he has the nuts-and-bolts information he needs. Later, when we have a chance to talk, I might elaborate on the humorous details of what occurred and my feelings about the situation.

Women tend to want to make a story out of everything. My daughter Marita has this tendency. She and her husband have the same personalities as Fred and me. Chuck will ask her, "Did the repairman come?" expecting a simple "yes" or "no" answer. Her response is, "Wait until I tell you." Then she launches into a hilarious description of her entire day, culminating in the repairman's actual visit. Her sanguine stories are not what he needs at the moment, but in Marita's mind it's no fun to say "yes" or "no." She prefers to give her husband a story complete with suspense and excitement, worthy of being published in book form.

As women, many of us prefer to express ourselves in emotional, colorful ways. However, if we hope to keep our husbands listening to us, it's worth tuning in to what style of communication a man responds to best.

Timing Is Everything

Like many women, I have the habit of telling too much too soon. Early in our marriage it wasn't uncommon for me to jump on Fred the minute he walked in the door and say, "We need to talk this minute. I've got a terrible problem." Immediately, I forced Fred to enter my crisis mode and, not surprisingly, he rarely responded with empathy.

Over the years, I've come to realize how important timing is in getting Fred to listen sensitively to me. Now, when I have something I want to discuss with him, I try to ask him when would be a good time for us to talk. Amazingly, quite often he will say, "If you'll just let me make this one phone call, then I'll have time." By letting him know it's important that we talk and giving him the option of deciding on a time, he's less preoccupied with other concerns and more willing to work through whatever issues face us.

———— ✑ ————

When I want to talk for the sake of verbalizing my feelings and connecting with Fred emotionally, I try to preface our conversation with, "I need to talk to you. I don't want an answer, I just want to share what I've been thinking about."

Even to this day, Fred has a hard time comprehending why someone wouldn't want a quick solution to a problem, but he's willing to accept my need to just be heard over his natural inclination to want to offer advice.

I KNOW HOW YOU FEEL

John is an eternal optimist. He sees the bright side of any question. Sometimes, while he's skimming along on the top of the lake, I'm plunging onto its depths. While I would never expect him to get depressed just because I am, what makes me feel close to him is when he acknowledges my feelings instead of giving answers, or saying, "Honey, tomorrow you'll feel better. I know you, your moods will change." There's nothing more reassuring than having someone say, "Yes, I hear you, I understand you, I'm with you, and I acknowledge that you're feeling bad."

—Luci

Filling in the Gaps

Getting Fred to listen for the sake of listening was a legitimate expectation of mine for our marriage. But expecting that he will truly understand my feelings is unreasonable. Because he is a man and we have two totally different personalities, Fred does not always comprehend why I react as I do to certain situations, just as I don't completely understand him.

At this point in our life, we have achieved a degree of emotional intimacy I never thought was possible. We have learned to listen without interrupting. We understand our personality differences. We are dedicated to meeting each other's emotional needs. We have grown closer to the Lord and therefore much closer to each other. We can now work side by side, seven days a week, twenty-four hours a day, and enjoy each other's company. Our marriage is evidence of what God can do when we use the tools He has made available.

Occasionally, when I wish to discuss something about which I need a female point of view, I call up a friend who will let me sputter on about my feelings and offer emotional support. Because our husbands cannot be everything for us, we are wise to cultivate other relationships that compensate for the voids that exist. While friends are a critical factor to most women's emotional health, we need to take care that the bond we develop with each other doesn't become a substitute for the intimacy we should share with our husbands. I've seen situations where two women do everything together and the husbands end up out in the cold.

Having endured several years of an emotional void in my marriage, I understand women who say they've given up trying to get their partner to listen. But what I've also learned by hanging in there is that if at least the wife tries to understand her mate and develop an awareness of his needs, the marriage has a good chance of not just surviving but of thriving. If we can learn to lower our expectations of our husbands where listening is concerned and try to tune in to their style of communicating, we may stand a greater chance of being heard.

So many of the riches Fred and I now share in our marriage weren't unearthed until the last few years. After plodding along, trying to express ourselves and understand each other, we're finally at the point where the effort is paying off. Though our personalities are still opposites, we seem to be balancing the differences better. I've learned to feel and think at the deeper level that comes so naturally for Fred, and likewise, he has picked up much of my spontaneity and excitement about life. We have come in from our extremes and met in the middle.

When I look back and see how close we were to giving up on our whole relationship, I realize how critical time is in allowing us to grow, heal, and mature. I encourage any woman struggling to find emotional intimacy in her marriage to hang in there long enough to discover it. And if you had that intimacy once, then take steps to recapture it. In all probability, your husband wants to understand you and feel close to you, he just may not know how. We have found that men who might not take the time to read about the personalities will instead listen to tapes in their car.

Make It Happen

1. Review the personality quiz at the end of chapter two. Do you see patterns in the way you and your spouse communicate? Does his personality and style of communicating help explain some of the problems you face when it comes to building emotional intimacy? Discuss your differences and consider ways you can reach a compromise. Spend some time in prayer, thanking God for the qualities you appreciate in your spouse and ask for eyes and a heart to learn to understand and love the differences.

2. If you have shut down emotionally from your husband, commit yourself to gradually opening up again. While you will feel vulnerable, set a goal of divulging one inner thought about yourself each day. Don't expect that each moment of sharing will evolve into meaningful conversation. Let your mate know how important it is to be able to share yourself with him so that you don't have to find someone else to talk to.

3. To get the conversational ball rolling again in your marriage start by asking questions—not probing, personal questions but fun questions like, "What was your most memorable summer as a child?" "In the past year, what was your favorite movie and why?" or "If you could visit any country in the world which one would it be and why?" Look for non-intimidating ice-breakers that can get you out of your daily conversational rut. Move your communication beyond "pass the salt."

SECTION THREE

MY PRIVATE BATTLES

AS CHRISTIANS, we're sometimes hesitant to admit when we feel lonely, guilty, or unhappy. We think we should be forever filled with happiness and on top of the world—never bothered by the more negative emotions. But before we're too hard on ourselves, we need to remember that God designed each of us to feel a range of emotions—from joy to sorrow, camaraderie to loneliness. Furthermore, following Christ doesn't negate the fact that we're human—the fact that we will experience the blues on occasion or feel disappointed when things don't go our way.

For some of us, certain emotions wage war on our soul. For instance, Annie says she tends to worry obsessively when she and her family travel. Luci has bouts of deep melancholy. Florence, since childhood, has done battle with feelings of envy and jealousy.

Rather than fight your emotional battles alone, challenge yourself as you read the following chapters to expose your struggles to the Lord and allow the insights and encouragement Annie, Florence, and Luci offer to penetrate your mind and heart. With their advice and the Lord's help, may you become the balanced and complete woman God created you to be.

8

Why Am I Sometimes Plagued With Guilt?

—*Florence Littauer*

I HAVE NEVER KNOWN a woman who wasn't plagued by guilt—real or imagined—at some point in her life. As women, we have a naturally heightened sensitivity toward others' needs and problems, so it's easy for us to become the emotional leader of the family. However, too often in our attempts to care for the emotional health of those around us, we inadvertently allow others to place the blame for their problems on us. And over time, as we absorb their guilt, we lose sight of who the guilty party truly is.

Unfortunately, many women haven't developed the skills to distinguish between true and false guilt, so we remain hostage to wrongful blame. We fall victim to the trap of internalizing all of the messages we're bombarded with to the point we can no longer discern whether we are guilty or innocent. For instance, how many times have you felt guilty when someone says, "I always attend an adult Bible study," or "I scrub my kitchen floor twice a week on my hands and knees"? We buy into others' judgments of what is right or wrong instead of deciding what is right or wrong based on our personal circumstances.

True or False Questions

Whenever we feel guilty, we are expending emotional energy. In most cases, our effort is wasted because we feel guilty when we shouldn't. To break free from habitually feeling guilty, the first step we need to develop is the ability to determine if our guilt is necessary or unnecessary.

Necessary guilt is the feeling that prompts us to make a right choice or realize we have made a mistake. For example, a woman may not feel like visiting her mother in the nursing home, but she knows it's something she needs to do. Her sense of guilt motivates her to go anyway, even when she'd rather not. Many times the Lord gives us a feeling of guilt so we'll do the right thing.

On the other hand, unnecessary guilt is that which makes us feel guilty when we aren't at fault. I knew a young woman once who was guilt-ridden over the fact that her mother had threatened to commit suicide. Her mother would say, "If you'd been a decent daughter, I wouldn't want to kill myself." As I worked with the woman, I helped her sort out whether or not she was feeling legitimate guilt. We listed all of the many loving things she did for her mother, including visiting her a number of times each week and calling her every morning. It seemed to me she was doing all one person could do for another person, but I said to her, "Ask the Lord if there is anything else you should be doing for your mother. If there is, then do it—regardless of how she responds. In this way, you will not hold any of the blame if she chooses to kill herself."

The woman followed my advice, and sadly, her mother did take her life. Later, I received a letter from the woman in which she said how grateful she was that she had dealt with the guilt ahead of time. Upon her mother's death she didn't feel guilty, because she knew she had done all she could.

FIGHTING THE FEVER

True guilt is like a fever—it shows us when something's wrong. It leads us to repentance. But then there's the other kind of guilt that wears you out—false guilt. For instance, I feel guilty when I don't use coupons in the grocery store. Everytime I go up to the checkout counter and the woman asks, "Do you have any coupons?" I feel obligated to explain my life to the cashier and why I haven't been able to clip and organize coupons this week. I shouldn't feel guilty about not having coupons.

—Annie

Erase the Guilt

Once we have decided if the guilt we feel is necessary (true) guilt or unnecessary (false) guilt, the second step is to purge ourselves of the negative feelings that dominate our lives. If the guilt you experience is legitimate, you need to confess your sin to God, seek His forgiveness, and try to rectify the situation where you can.

In the past I struggled with the need for approval and love. Subconsciously I would try to meet this need by sensationalizing stories so others would find me interesting. Many times I've realized upon embroidering on an incident or dramatizing an event that what I've said went beyond the truth. Guilt helps me recognize my sin for what it is. The guilt I feel is God telling me to watch my words and make sure I speak the truth. When I discover I've embellished a story, I go to the person to whom I was speaking and say, "What I said wasn't entirely factual. I exaggerated. Will you forgive me?" It is only by forgiveness that our guilt leaves us and we are free again. Fred and I now laugh at some of my past stories and realize that they were practice for my messages of hope and humor today.

When false guilt is involved, the steps to purging ourselves of our guilt feelings are often more drastic. If your life is plagued by unnecessary guilt, it may be time to place blame where blame is due. I feel that there are times when we have the right to take the offensive, especially if it is our mate who continually makes us feel guilty. Experience has shown me that when the woman is strong enough to say, "I'm not going to live this way any longer. Your putting me down and blaming me for your problems is not honoring to the Lord," husbands are usually willing to work at change. Most of us don't like confronting others, even when their behavior hurts us. I believe it's especially hard for Christian women to confront a spouse.

At one point in my marriage, my daughter and I, along with an outside party, confronted Fred about some anger that was affecting our family. Initially, he felt as though he was under attack and our accusations were invalid. Thankfully, because he is a deeply spiritual person, Fred came to realize his faulty behavior patterns. Because Fred writes his prayers each day, the confrontation led him to bring our comments to the Lord, search his heart for confirmation, and examine his family background to uncover the roots of his anger. Once the Lord showed him the buried abuse, he was relieved to know the truth. For as it says in John 8:32, "the truth will set you free." Indeed, once Fred knew the truth, the anger disappeared.

Though confrontation is not the first choice for transferring guilt to the proper person, what often convicts a woman to go this route is the fact that her situation will not improve unless she takes action. When I work with a woman who is grappling with the decision to confront her mate, I have her ask herself, "Will the confrontation solve anything?" and "Will it be a positive step in our relationship?" If a woman suspects her husband will scream or physically abuse her, then confrontation may not be the right solution at that time. However, if she believes a confrontation is necessary and is the only way to free herself of false guilt and get her mate to take responsibility for his actions, then I suggest having a third party present during the confrontation.

If a woman decides against confronting her mate, I challenge her to consider what her life will be like ten years down the road. I ask her to consider whether she is making the right choice spiritually by allowing her husband to continually make her feel guilty and placing the responsibility on her for his emotional problems.

While confronting Fred wasn't easy, the benefits that came from taking this route can be seen in our marriage today. We now have a depth of relationship and a sense of understanding that we never had before.

COMING CLEAN

Guilt comes from perceived failure. But there is false guilt as well as true shame and guilt. Ask God to show you which is yours, and how to right the wrong that has led to real guilt.

—*Luci*

Listening to God

A third step in unraveling our tangled emotions, especially where guilt is concerned, is "listening prayer."

Listening prayer is a way of freeing your mind so that God can speak to you and reveal whatever burdens are keeping you from a full relationship with Him or others. When Fred and I teach our seminars, we have our students write a letter to the Lord. It might go like this:

> Dear Lord Jesus,
> When I think about the situation I'm in today, this is how I feel about it. As I look in my background to come up with the reason why I feel this way, I don't have an answer. I'm awaiting what you want me to know.

After you've written some thoughts, sit quietly, pen in hand. Then, write down whatever thoughts come into your mind. Fred and I have been amazed by the way the Lord starts speaking when you open your mind to Him and begin to record the thoughts He reveals to you. The students can hardly contain their excitement over having the Lord directly speak to them. Most likely, though, they've never heard Him because they haven't taken the time to listen.

A close friend describes listening prayers as follows: "If I went over to visit Florence one afternoon, sat down, and told her everything that had happened to me in the last two weeks, and as soon as I got to the end of my story I said, 'Well, thanks for listening. Good-bye!' how would Florence feel? She'd think, 'Wait, I didn't have a chance to respond.' " That's the way it is with God. Too often we say, "Lord, here's my problem," and then we shut the door and expect Him to break it down and force us to listen. God doesn't do that. We need to allow Him time to speak.

Listening prayer also helps us bring specific concerns or problems to the Lord, so we can hone in on certain trouble spots, such as guilt. So many times we offer generic prayers to God like, "My marriage is terrible. Fix it." What God wants is for us to come to him with the specifics and say, "Lord, I've spent some time on this. I know that I have a guilt problem. Why do I have it?" Then listen. Write down what He says. Think about it. Pray about it. Be specific. The Lord will clean up the garbage in our life, but He'll only take away the trash that we put out.

Many times I'll talk with someone who has obvious emotional problems that tie into their feelings of guilt. Yet, when I ask that person if she wants to get to the root of her guilt, she declines. "What if I find out that it was my father who made me feel so guilty?" she might argue. When we are traumatized as children, often we push the painful memories into our subconscious. When this is the case, it may be scary to engage in listening prayer and difficult to know where to start. But I encourage the person to dig up the source of her guilty feelings and present her memories to Christ so He can begin to heal her.

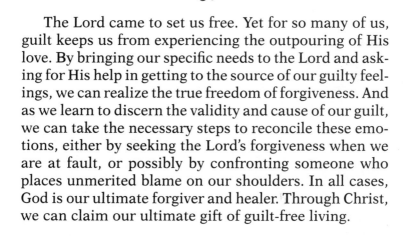

The Lord came to set us free. Yet for so many of us, guilt keeps us from experiencing the outpouring of His love. By bringing our specific needs to the Lord and asking for His help in getting to the source of our guilty feelings, we can realize the true freedom of forgiveness. And as we learn to discern the validity and cause of our guilt, we can take the necessary steps to reconcile these emotions, either by seeking the Lord's forgiveness when we are at fault, or possibly by confronting someone who places unmerited blame on our shoulders. In all cases, God is our ultimate forgiver and healer. Through Christ, we can claim our ultimate gift of guilt-free living.

Make It Happen

1. If you frequently feel a sense of guilt, try engaging in listening prayer. Bring before the Lord your expec-

tations and your sense of guilt when you fail to meet them. If the expectations you didn't meet are God's expectations, then ask for His forgiveness and strength to follow through in the future. If the expectations are self-imposed or from others, then carefully weed through them looking for areas where you're setting yourself up for a sense of false guilt.

2. Often people who are plagued by unnecessary guilt are those who struggle with a low self-esteem. As you react to different situations throughout each day, try to discern where your guilt stems from. Are you a people-pleaser instead of a God-pleaser? Do you doubt yourself and your own opinions when others challenge you? Ask God to give you a spirit of confidence and meditate on Scripture, such as Psalm 139, that expresses the value that God places on you.

3. Challenge the "shoulds" in your life. The next time you find yourself saying, "I should do this," examine the foundations of your "should." Is it an expectation from your upbringing that has little bearing on your life as an adult? Is it from the media or friends? You'll be surprised how many of your "shoulds" are really unrealistic and often irrelevant expectations traveling in disguise.

9

How Can I Move Beyond the Sadness Associated With Loss?

—Luci Shaw

A FEW OF MY FRIENDS deliberately decided not to marry, or, if they married, not to have children. Instead, they chose a life of convenience and comfort as well as the freedom to travel. Now that these friends are in their sixties, they are noticing the joys of children—and especially grandchildren—enjoyed by others who chose to marry and/or have a family. My single friends are beginning to experience a deep sense of loss from missing out on these opportunities.

Yes, they have enjoyed the benefits of a lifestyle free from the demands of growing children. They may also have greater financial resources. However, the new challenge for them is to deal with the grief they are experiencing and move beyond the point of regret.

All of us know the sadness and pain related to the road not taken or the journey suddenly cut short. When my first husband, Harold, died, I thought I would never feel whole again. After nearly thirty-three years of marriage, I felt as though part of me died with Harold. Death, though perhaps the ultimate loss, is only one of the many losses each of us will face in our lives. Divorce, blighted friendships, moves, career changes—all of these events elicit a sense of loss, especially for women.

Along with grieving the big changes in life, we also tend to feel a loss over the smaller choices and events that comprise our lives—having two children instead of three, or losing a prized possession. While men grieve over the same kinds of losses, women tend to experience loss more frequently and more deeply than men. As women, we tend to attach ourselves emotionally to the people and things around us and in the process give each facet of our lives more meaning.

For instance, I may value a ceramic salad bowl that my husband gave me, not because it's particularly rare or expensive, but simply because it was his gift to me. The presence of that bowl reinforces my relationship with my husband. If that bowl were to break, I would mourn the loss because a small part of what makes up our relationship is lost. Granted, grieving over a broken bowl is very different than mourning the death of a spouse, but both losses elicit feelings of sadness. How, then, can we learn to move beyond the intense emotional reaction we experience from a loss?

Feel the Pain

To move beyond our feelings of loss we first need to allow ourselves to feel the pain. I couldn't expect to be free from sadness and pain six months after Harold died. I needed time, in my case three to four years, to come to terms with all that his death meant for me emotionally, physically, and spiritually. For me, grieving was a slow process, but I felt it was better to heal thoroughly and deal with the pain, allowing the wound to heal rather than put on a serene face (like a Band-Aid) and pretend everything was fine. I needed to work through the loss rather than dodge it or distract myself from it.

A friend taught me it's okay to let the deep pain hurt. Don't try to anesthetize it. The pain is reality; it has a work to do in us. It teaches us a new reality about life and death—truths we need to face. Only in that context of acknowledging our pain can we truly heal and become whole persons again.

WORKING THROUGH THE STAGES

Whether you've experienced a job loss or the death of a child or spouse, every loss needs to be processed through the same four steps of grieving: denial, anger, acceptance, and, finally, resolution. It's helpful to remember these stages so that when you're going through the grieving process and you get to the point where you're angry at God, you don't also burden yourself with the guilty thought that you are a failure as a Christian. All of these stages are normal and they all will pass.

—Florence

Life is a journey, and obviously some of the journey is going to be painful. There are ways to use the losses in life as avenues for growth rather than resent them as obstacles. My journal was an immense help in working through my grief and pain after Harold died. By writing down everything I was feeling—all the loss, the blankness, the sensation of being cut in half—I could see my emotions on the page for what they were. My journal made my loss more manageable. On paper I could better see the shape and size of my grief and wasn't as likely to feel overwhelmed by it. Several times the deep, emotional pain I felt was so strong I didn't think I could bear it. Then I would write it all out, and, in the process, much of the pain was drawn out of me.

My journal became a way to gauge my growth, showing me that I was making measurable progress. Each entry represents a day's progress along my path of life, and gives me tangible evidence that I'm moving ahead even when I don't feel as if I am.

Let Go of the Loss

Sometimes the losses we experience seem bigger than we are. Try as we may, we can't seem to overcome them. The feeling of loss just keeps looming over us and we can't seem to get beyond the point of grief that comes in overwhelming waves. At this juncture, the only solution is to put ourselves into God's hands.

About six months after Harold died, a spiritual counselor said to me, "You've been through a long, dark tunnel. You're coming out into the light now, and you're going to find yourself on the edge of a cliff. You need to throw yourself off the cliff and trust that God will catch you."

While I believed him at a profound level, I didn't know *how* I was to throw myself off this metaphorical cliff. Soon after, I was traveling in Vancouver and somehow lost my journal—the record of my deepest struggles and emotions during the preceding six months. I felt as if I had lost part of myself. Then I realized that God was saying, "This is one way you can abandon yourself to me. You can let go of your journal and say, 'I give it to you.'" It wasn't easy, but I said "Yes" to God right at that moment. I knew I had no alternative. I had to be willing to let my journal go.

Later that afternoon, a friend was driving along the same busy street in Vancouver and she noticed a notebook lying in a puddle. She stopped, picked it up, and saw my name and address on the cover, and quickly returned my lost journal to me that afternoon!

In this process of relinquishment, God gave me back what He knew was important to me. But the critical lesson I learned was not to cling so tightly to my losses. Almost every loss is balanced by a corresponding gain in another area. If we're willing to let go of a loss, God will give back to us what we have let go, with an additional sense of himself being personally involved in our lives. That is certainly what I experienced the day I lost my journal. I have a richness with God I never would have had without the loss. The gain was worth the pain of relinquishment.

Humans want to be in control. For Christians particularly, the crunch comes when we want to hold onto control of our lives, something that truly belongs in God's hands. It takes turning a corner, as I experienced with my journal, to allow God to have control.

Halfway through my grieving process over Harold's death, I realized one of my defense mechanisms against chaos—both the inner turmoil that comes with death and bereavement, and the practical (legal and financial) matters that overwhelmed me—was to organize my life so that I knew exactly where to find any information I needed. I filed everything, made lists, cleaned my drawers and organized my books, my kitchen, my desk. I became obsessed with order. I finally recognized that I had to let go of this need to be in total control—both figuratively and literally—and let God order my life.

Share the Pain

Since I've moved out to California I've become part of a prayer group of five women. Each woman in the group is involved in some type of public Christian ministry. For me, this group has been an enormous relief because here I can let down barriers and be myself. Unlike when I'm in public, I don't have to appear to be in control and always have the right answers. With these women I can cry, acknowledge failure, or confess sin without losing any of my value to them. In fact, we each gain value in our honesty and sense of compassion for each other. To hear others say, "Oh, I feel the same way," or "I went through that," helps me put my personal losses into perspective. I begin to realize that even though I may feel an intense emotion right now, the woman next to me has gone through the same experience and survived. There's a lot to be said for mutuality of experience.

Even if you're not in a prayer group or support group, it's important to let others bear your losses and burdens with you. So many times while Harold was dying and after his death, my friends were Christ to me. Ironically, during this period I struggled with the reality of Christ and often I failed to recognize that the Lord was coming to me in specific and tangible ways through the people who came into my life and loved me. With hindsight, I can see how God was making himself known to me and carrying my burdens through the love of the people around me.

GOD OF THE GOOD

In times of sadness and loss, ultimately we must understand God is in control. Whatever comes to me comes through His loving hand. Once we can see God as all-loving, then, and only then, can we look for the good He brings from loss. I once read a quote attributed to Warren Wiersbe that said, "When God permits His children to go through the furnace, He keeps His eye on the clock and His hand on the thermostat. His loving heart knows how much and how long."

—Annie

Most of us perceive loss as a negative experience, something that happens to us that is beyond our control. I am beginning to realize there are some things worth losing because I know my loss will eventually be offset by an even greater gain. For instance, as the years pass, I don't have the boundless energy I once had; I'm not as thin as I used to be; my skin doesn't have the same firmness and elasticity. For many women, aging introduces one of the most difficult losses of all to accept, especially in a culture that prizes youth and beauty. Coming to terms with our physical selves or any type of loss can cause us to feel a great sense of sadness. Yet until we see the losses in our lives as part of God's bigger picture as He welcomes us into eternity, our eyes will remain captured and focused on the temporal—the here and now. We need to see beyond this life and realize that anything we lose in this world is going to be rewarded in far greater proportion in the life to come. I'm trying to get my eyes off how I look and feel and move into that larger realm—what, in my life, has *lasting* value?

Losses truly are a part of life. And though I may have lost—and continue to lose—big and little things now, they're really nothing in comparison with what I'm going to gain.

Make It Happen

1. If you're struggling with some loss in your life, start keeping a journal to record your feelings. Allow yourself to express your pain, anger, and sadness. As you write down questions, struggles, and pains, offer your words to God as a prayer. Periodically, review what you have written to discover the progress you've made.

2. If, after a loss, sadness and depression continue to dominate your life, professional counseling may be in order. Consider joining a local support group or prayer group at your church as well. Ask others to share your burdens through prayer.

3. If the loss you have experienced has made you doubt the reality of Christ in your life, make a list of all

the blessings you have experienced related to the loss you have suffered. Some blessings may be as small and seemingly insignificant as seeing the sun shine on a day when you were feeling down. Don't discount any of the small but precious and intimate ways God tells you He is with you.

10

How Do I Keep Disappointment From Robbing Me of a Sense of Joy?

—Annie Chapman

THE VAN IS PACKED. Favorite books and tapes are neatly stacked in plastic milk crates and carefully placed in the corner out of the way. Pillows and blankets are spread, ready for the children to crawl in quickly and go back to sleep. Excitement is high—we're going to Grandma's house. An undeniable feeling of happiness propels us along as we prepare for points north. However, our feelings of happiness have everything to do with what is happening at the time.

Two hours later, the kids are awake, the toys and books are scattered about, the blankets are wadded-up messes, and the familiar whine of, "How much longer till we get there?" fills the air. For the duration of our eight-hour trip, our happiness gives way to a more practical, long-enduring sense of joy.

Joy has little or nothing to do with what's happening. It has everything to do with the purpose of the journey. Joy is knowing that after a long journey the reward will be arriving at Grandma's safely.

And so it is in the journey of life. Happiness doesn't

get us very far on its own. It's too contingent on happenings, and happenings are always changing. Joy, on the other hand, is a sense of purpose and destiny. We know that despite what happens to us day by day, God is still with us, helping us fulfill His ultimate purpose for our lives.

In spite of this truth, all of us feel joy-less at times. What often steals our joy is disappointment over a minor aggravation that leaves us disheartened or a forceful blow that leaves us emotionally paralyzed for years. Either way, disappointment is an inevitable part of life, and we need to learn how to deal with it if we hope to prevent it from robbing us of joy.

Assess Your Expectations

The source of our disappointment is most often a sense of unmet expectations. Webster's Dictionary defines disappointment as: "To fail to satisfy the hopes or expectations of; to break one's promise."

When I gave birth to my daughter, Heidi, I wasn't disappointed that Nancy Reagan didn't come to see me and bring a tuna casserole. I didn't expect her to. But I was disappointed when my best friend didn't come to see me or help me with my housework. I thought she would because I had done the same for her when she experienced a miscarriage. I expected her to be there for me. When she wasn't, I was disappointed.

To restore joy in our lives we need to reassess our expectations, particularly of others. God did not intend for us to find our significance through others. Beyond reassessing our expectations, at times we need to let our disappointment over unmet expectations be known so they don't lead to sin.

Recently Heidi and I, along with her girl friend, visited my parents over spring break. When we returned from our long drive home, I subconsciously expected

Steve to be waiting for us. I also expected the house to be clean. When I arrived, however, Steve was out fishing. He had cleaned fish in the sink and left a smelly mess in the garbage. There was mud on the kitchen table, and the bed was unmade. Then I found his note: "Hi. Glad you're home. I've gone fishing. I'll be back at dark." I was so disappointed he wasn't home that I immediately flew into a rage and got mad at everybody. That's how disappointment works—expectation turns to disappointment, which turns to anger, which turns to hostile/aggressive behavior. And when disappointment leads us to sin in this way, we need to seek forgiveness for our misplaced anger.

WHAT MATTERS TO ME

One of my biggest problems has been accepting the disappointing performances from others who don't happen to share my excitement over a given project. Understanding the basic personalities has helped me to realize that many do not have my natural enthusiasm. So now when I'm disappointed, I shrug it off and acknowledge, "Just because they're different doesn't make them wrong."

—Florence

When Steve got home that night, the first thing Heidi said was, "Mom's been mad at you all afternoon." He looked at me with surprise and confusion. Rather than rail against him angrily and irrationally, I said, "You had no idea what I expected, but this is what I thought I would come home to: I expected you to be here waiting to greet me with open arms, and I thought the house would be clean. I missed you."

Had I spent all day thinking, "If he really loved me

he could read my mind," as I once did as a newlywed, I would have wallowed in pity and Steve never would have known why. By letting Steve understand my disappointment and how it turned to anger, he and I both learned how detrimental disappointment from unmet expectations can be in a relationship and to our sense of joy.

Make a Choice

Naturally we're disappointed when things don't go as expected, but when we face a disappointment, we also have a choice. We can wallow in self-pity and despair, moving further from joy, or we can walk hand-in-hand with God trusting His plan for us.

Joseph of Egypt understood this choice. He is a sterling example of a person who faced unfairness, extreme hardship, unmet expectations, betrayal, and rejection, and yet he never lost sight of God's destiny for him. While he experienced great disappointment, he never lost his sense of joy. He chose to continue serving God despite the rotten turns his life took rather than surrender to self-pity. Because of his choice, he ultimately accomplished God's intended purpose.

Some friends of mine faced a similar choice. Teresa and William were anticipating the birth of their second child. They followed the doctor's orders to the letter and expected a healthy baby. However, their son was born undersized. He was placed in an incubator, but someone mistakenly gave him too much oxygen causing him to go blind. Next he lost his hearing, and finally he became paralyzed. Everything that could have gone wrong did.

As Teresa looked in the nursery at all the healthy babies, she knew she had a choice to make. She could stand there and wish her baby was whole, or she could choose the harder path and reach out, take God's hand, and walk His way of sorrow. Both choices would lead to death—one path, the death of her soul and spirit from self-pity and grief; the other path, the death of self.

She chose to walk the Lord's way, knowing that even though she made the right choice, the hurt and bitterness that accompany such terrible disappointment would not automatically disappear. For the next nine months my friends watched as their son deteriorated and eventually died. Their disappointment was undeniable, but if they chose to continue to dwell on the baseball games that would never be played, they would have lost sight of the joy God intended for them.

Disappointment makes us want to give up. But despair is Satan's ploy to keep us from living joyfully. Just as Joseph of Egypt and my friends Teresa and William had to make a conscious decision not to despair, so must we when faced with devastating setbacks. If you've tried to have a baby and can't, battle it out with God. That's what Hannah did. She didn't throw a pity party. 1 Samuel 1:6–7 says, "And because the LORD had closed her womb, her rival kept provoking her in order to irritate her. This went on year after year. Whenever Hannah went up to the house of the LORD, her rival provoked her till she wept and would not eat." The rival in this account was Hannah's husband's other wife, but our enemy is really the attacker of our soul—Satan. He torments us when we're down, disappointed, and depressed. Instead of allowing ourselves to be beaten up by him, we need to go to God and have it out like Hannah eventually did.

Foster a Thankful Heart

Many of us expect God to bless us with health, wealth, and happiness. We expect to live long lives, have happy marriages, and raise wonderful children. We expect to be grandparents, have money, or be smart. The flip side of our disappointments, however, is gratitude for all of the gifts God has given us. Yet, too many of us fail to be content with what we have. Ingratitude is the cornerstone of disappointment, and the only way to re-build a foundation for joyful living is to begin to thank God continually in every situation. Like the apostle Paul says in Philippians 4:11–13, "I have learned to be con-tent whatever the circumstances. I know what it is to be in need, and I know what it is to have plenty. I have learned the secret of being content in any and every sit-uation, whether well fed or hungry, whether living in plenty or in want. I can do everything through him who gives me strength."

WITHIN GOD'S PLAN

Joy comes from the realization that we are living in the center of God's plan for us. Disappointment often focuses on the failure of our own agenda rather than God's long-term purposes for us, which may use stress and struggle as tools for strengthening our spiritual muscles. Develop a kind of spiritual farsightedness, which recognizes our selfish purposes and God's purposes.

—Luci

Proverbs 30:8–9 also helps in refocusing our thoughts on trusting in God's provision rather than our own selfish expectations: "Give me neither poverty nor riches, but give me only my daily bread. Otherwise, I may have too much and disown you and say, 'Who is the Lord?' Or I may become poor and steal, and so dishonor the name of my God." When we wish we had what others have, we're really saying that what God has given us isn't good enough. We need to replace distrust and ingratitude with thanksgiving. 1 John 2:15–17 says, "Do not love the world or anything in the world. If anyone loves the world, the love of the Father is not in him. For everything in the world—the cravings of sinful man, the lust of his eyes and the boasting of what he has and does—comes not from the Father but from the world. The world and its desires will pass away, but the man who does the will of God will live forever."

Abraham Lincoln's life was one full of disappointments. In 1831, he failed in business. In 1832, he was defeated for legislature. In 1833, again, he failed in business. In 1834, he was elected to the legislature. In 1835, his sweetheart died, and the following year he had a nervous breakdown. He was defeated for office three times between 1838 and 1843. In 1846, he was elected to Congress only to be defeated in his re-election attempt two years later. Twice he was defeated for Senate before he was finally elected President in 1860.

Lincoln failed more times than he succeeded. But in all cases he proved that neither success nor failure is permanent. So it is with the many disappointments we will face in life. Whether we succeed or fail is not important, but rather that we're doing the Lord's will. It is our journey that counts—that is what gives us joy. Despite our disappointments, we can know in God's eyes we are succeeding. And with this eternal perspective, our disappointments will not rob us of our joy.

Make It Happen

1. If you struggle with ingratitude, read and memorize Scripture passages that talk about being content, such as 1 Timothy 6:6 and Job 36:11. Put your awareness of all the blessings you have received into action by

reaching out to others who may not have as much as you.

2. If anger, despair, or depression have moved in to your life where joy used to dwell, take stock of your expectations. Review the relationships, accomplishments, or situations that disappoint you, and spend some time sorting through your feelings. Offer your hurts to God and ask Him to heal you and turn your sadness into joy.

3. Disappointments can range from minor losses, like not getting the promotion you had hoped for, to major setbacks, like discovering your son is homosexual. God cares about each of our disappointments whether large or small. For insight into handling disappointment, especially disappointment with God, read the book of Job. What common threads run through Job's feelings of disappointment versus yours? And how does Job deal with his feelings?

How Content Are You?
Kathy Collard Miller

Our culture tells us "more" will make us happy—and if we believe its lies, God's special gift of contentment can slip from our grasp. Here are two major contentment cheaters and how you can overcome them.

Perfectionism

Someone has said that a perfectionist is a person who takes great pains—then passes them on to others. Before you conclude that description doesn't apply to you, take this quiz developed by Sandra Simpson LeSourd in her book, *The Compulsive Woman* (Chosen Books). Check the statements that apply to you:

- If I can't do something exactly right, I won't do it at all.
- I often start things I don't finish.
- It's hard for me to relax even after my work is done.
- I am often amazed at the incompetence of others.
- I can't stand it when things are out of place.
- I find unpredictability vexing, if not intolerable.
- I have a burning need to set things right.
- I worry a lot about why I haven't done better.
- Any kind of personal failure is the worst thing I can think of.
- It seems to me that standards are slipping everywhere.

If three or more of those statements apply to you, you have perfectionistic tendencies and contentment may be a difficult goal for you to attain.

While it is true that God wants us to be continually growing into the image of Jesus Christ, the good news for discontented perfectionists is that God already views us as perfect in our position in Christ. Hebrews 10:14 tells us, "Because by one sacrifice he has made perfect forever those who are being made holy." God already loves and accepts us as much as He possibly can—even as He prunes the ungodly portions from our lives.

When speaking at women's retreats, I urge perfectionists to think in terms of "One percent improvement." Perfectionists often lack contentment because they only value one-hundred percent growth. Yet we never reach such a high standard. Instead, as we begin to ask God and be grateful for even one percent progress in an area, it'll be easier for us to be content—and successful!

Materialism

About 100 years ago, a survey asked average Americans to list their wants—they listed seventy. In a similar survey, Americans recently listed 500. How naturally I fall victim to the contentment cheater called materialism. "Oh, I must have that dress. I need it!" The Lord gently taps my mental shoulder and inquires, "Kathy, you need that dress? Will you die without it?" I want to say, "Yes!" but I know it's not true. How easily I use the word "need" when it's really a "want."

Television commercials bombard us with "New!" and "Improved!" Its subtle message: we can't be content without the newest fashions or the most expensive car. Battered by the messages of the media, we conclude that needs and wants are the same, and contentment sadly hangs its head and backs out the door.

Let's welcome it back by facing the contentment cheater of materialism and shouting, "God promises to meet all my true needs and is so generous, He often gives me my wants!" Philippians 4:19 is our watchword: "And my God will meet all your needs according to his glorious riches in Christ Jesus."

Sometimes I wish that verse said, "God promises to supply

all your wants," but God knows best, and His wisdom can determine my true needs and my fickle wants. Even when God gives me my wants, I've noticed how quickly they lose their value. Only focusing my eyes on the Lord and heaven's future glories keeps me content with this temporal, unsatisfying world. Storing up treasures in heaven and building my character are far more worthy goals than maintaining the world's definition of "needs."

—From *Today's Christian Woman* (January/February 1992)

11

Why Do I Sometimes Feel Lonely?

—Luci Shaw

WHEN I FIRST MOVED out to California, my life was jammed with activities. Because of commitments made months and years before, I traveled, taught, and wrote as much as my schedule would allow. Yet, though my time was filled, I felt lonely. Aside from my husband, I had practically no kindred spirits to connect with on a deep emotional, intellectual, or artistic level. To feel fulfilled and complete, I needed to be in touch with people who value the same things as I do—namely fellow writers or artists. Until I'd made these connections, I felt as though I was in alien territory.

Many women echo this same tension. Even though their lives are swelling with activities, the inner desires of their hearts go unfulfilled, and they are left with an emptiness for which no amount of busyness can compensate. Granted, keeping busy distracts us from dwelling on the loneliness we feel, but it's not an antidote. The only way to truly overcome the inner void we feel is by actively cultivating relationships that meet our need to connect with others on a deep level.

Making Contact

Ideally the primary friendships to nurture are those within our own families—our husbands and children. Obviously, if my husband and I have enough interests in common, we'll enjoy each other's companionship and develop an intimacy based on our shared interests.

The same is true with children. As adults they are free to develop a new relationship with us, their parents, which can be a rewarding source of closeness. As my children reached adulthood and established their own lives, they gradually came back to develop a new relationship with me, not so much as their mother but as their friend, their peer. Now, I can truly say my children are my best friends.

Sadly, many women don't experience emotional intimacy with their spouses, or they remain at odds with their children. If this is the case, you may have to work at cultivating other friendships to satisfy your need for companionship and closeness. Remember that no one human is capable of meeting all our needs.

For instance, John has scores of friends. He's a gregarious person, the kind of guy everybody loves. We do a lot of entertaining in our home and often I'm surrounded by people he knows. However, John's friends are not necessarily the ones I would choose as my intimates. Rather than feel left out of his world because of our different needs for friendship, I began to develop my own circle of friends. One vital group of friends has been the prayer group of five professional women with whom I meet every two weeks. As I mentioned earlier, within this group we are free to be ourselves, to share our thoughts and ideas heart to heart. The loneliness I sometimes experience automatically drops away when I'm with this special group of friends.

Finding kindred spirits doesn't automatically happen. Often it takes intentional effort. At the church I belonged to in the Chicago suburbs, I felt a need to connect with people on an artistic level. I knew there were like-minded artists, writers, and musicians in our congregation who were striving to improve their talents, but I didn't know how to meet them. One Sunday, I asked permission to announce that anyone who was interested in forming a creative support group was welcome to meet at my house for a potluck supper that night. Thirty-six people showed up. The kindred spirits were out there, but it took an intentional move to pull us together.

An old proverb says, "He (she) who wants friends must show himself (herself) friendly." We have to reach out and be what the other person needs if we want a similar response in return. It's a two-way street; we can't expect friendship just to come to us. Yet it takes courage to open up and allow ourselves to be seen as we truly are and risk rejection. The only way to connect on an emotional level, though, is to stop hiding behind a false persona and allow ourselves to be transparent and real. Until we reach the place where we're communicating with our hearts and souls—and that means our conversations get beyond the weather, kids, food, or politics—loneliness will continue to pervade our lives.

FOR ONE ANOTHER

In Genesis, even though God surrounded Adam with His creation, Adam sensed a void until Eve was present. The desire to be known and loved is implanted by God. It's an innate drive to make us reach out to people.

—Annie

One Isn't Always the Loneliest Number

Most of us think of being alone as a negative. After Harold died, I realized that being alone didn't necessarily mean I was lonely. I came to enjoy the advantages of only having to care for myself at the end of a long day. If I was hungry, I could eat what I wanted, when I wanted. I could sleep when my body decided it needed rest. There was definitely a relief in not having to justify myself and my actions to anyone else!

It was during this time of freedom that I learned the difference between loneliness and solitude. Solitude is finding a wholeness, a completeness, a richness within myself. I value solitude because I'm a busy person, and I'm involved in many people's lives. I'm energized by people, but I'm also energized and recharged by being alone. For me, solitude means enjoying my own company because I feel self-contained and contented. Loneliness, on the other hand, comes when I recognize a lack of resources within myself. When I'm lonely, I want to reach out and make contact with other people because within myself I feel inadequate.

I didn't realize my own spiritual and emotional inadequacies until after Harold died. He was always such a strong, giving person, and whenever I would have difficulties or questions, I would confide in him and find understanding and comfort. When he died, I lost my human intermediary, and I was forced to go to God directly. In many ways, loneliness served a critical purpose in my spiritual development. It wasn't until I began to bring all of my needs to God that I began to see how He truly does fill every void.

Claiming God's presence and actually feeling it are two separate issues. I spent many months asking God to fill my heart's desires before I began to see He really was there for me. Now, when I look back in my journal, I realize that in a larger sense, God was there caring for me and planning my life all along—I just didn't realize it at the time. There is no sure-fire formula for achieving intimacy with God, but as long as our hearts are crying out for a close relationship with Him, we can be confident He will satisfy us in His own time.

STICK TO A SCHEDULE

When my mother lived in housing for the elderly, she disciplined herself to follow a schedule every day as a means to battle loneliness. By planning simple tasks for herself, the regimen brought purpose to her daily life and kept her from becoming aimless.

—Florence

Loneliness and a sense of lack isn't always a bad thing. It reminds us that life is a series of losses and gains—light and darkness. Just as a tree needs the stresses of the elements, such as wind and rain and drought, so, too, we need the stresses of life to mature. We need loneliness to appreciate the blessings we do have. And if we allow ourselves to absorb the feeling of loneliness and reflect on the experience, God can use it to teach us many new things about ourselves and about Him.

Make It Happen

1. Reflect on the areas in your life that do not meet the fullness and richness you desire. Prayerfully consider the ways God might want you to redeem the time you have and the loneliness you feel, whether it be to challenge yourself to make contact with others, or to

spend more time in intimate communion with God.

2. Sometimes having too much time on our hands breeds a need for more meaningful contact. Consider ways to reach out to others, especially those who are chronically lonely, like the elderly in nursing homes, or those who are homebound.

3. The next time you feel lonely, stop to analyze why you are experiencing this emotion. Is there a pattern to your loneliness? Do certain events or inadequacies within you trigger the need to be with others?

Lonely Hearts
Eileen Silva Kindig

Of all the factors contributing to loneliness, psychologists tell us one of the most crucial is lack of self-esteem. When we don't feel confident about our ability to find or accept love, it's difficult to reach out for the emotional connections we desire. For some, loneliness is a temporary condition triggered by a move, divorce, or the death of someone close. Sometimes even the most emotionally healthy peopie find themselves thrust into situations that force them to go it alone for a while. Chances are, if they feel good about themselves, eventually they'll bounce back. However, for others, loneliness is a condition that can haunt for a lifetime.

Lack of self-esteem also can keep us lonely within the very relationships that are supposed to bring us joy and fulfillment. When we don't feel worthy, we passively accept relationships that fail to meet our emotional needs, rather than actively improve them.

When poor self-esteem creates lonely places in our lives or prevents us from springing back from situational losses, we need to take a hard look at ourselves. Are we lonely to the point of feeling depressed, worthless, hopeless? If so, professional help may be needed.

Never Alone

When we realize on a deep, personal level that God created us and loves us—warts and all—we come to believe that with God in our lives we are never alone. Isaiah 43:5 (NKJV) begins: "Fear not, for I am with you."

151

Our faith, however, does not allow us to stop here. We need others to make our lives whole, but before we can become vulnerable to the give and take of an intimate relationship, we need to know who we are and be comfortable with ourselves. That means learning to be happily alone.

In the early days of Christianity, solitude was revered. Today we want our silences filled with sound. How we spend our time alone is as unique as each one of us, but at its finest, solitude is a gift we give ourselves. My best times of solitude are spent journaling, reading, or simply sitting on our family room couch with a cup of tea, taking in the splendor of the lake beyond our sliding glass doors.

Author Anne Morrow Lindbergh described it perfectly when she wrote, "I find there is a quality to being alone that is incredibly precious. Life rushes back into the void, richer, more vivid, fuller than before."

Centered on Others

Even though we can and should treasure our solitary moments, we still need others. That's why it's so important to give as well as receive. The founders of numerous self-help groups have wisely structured their programs around this concept of giving. Support groups for the widowed and divorced or phone groups for agoraphobics (people who fear open spaces), are all based on the concept of reaching out to others from the core of our own pain and isolation. Not only does it bring healing to those who are ministered to, but also to those who minister.

When we're cut off from others, we begin to lose a sense of who we are. But when others love us, think we're funny, smart, warm, or dependable, we grow in confidence and intimacy. To bring these blessings into our lives, we need to look to God, ourselves, and others. In them we find our way out of the darkness of loneliness.

—From *Today's Christian Woman* (September/October 1989)

12
Will I Always Battle Envy and Jealousy?

—*Florence Littauer*

THROUGHOUT MY CHILDHOOD, my entire family slept in one room behind my father's store. My bed was against the same wall as the cash register, and each night, after my parents closed shop, I'd hear them counting the day's receipts. Invariably, my mother would ask, "Will there be enough money to eat next week?" Looking back, I now understand why money and others' material possessions were a source of envy for me. Having grown up with so little, whenever I saw someone who had a big car or a large house, I would covet what they had.

Fred, on the other hand, grew up with all the material comforts I never knew, and I doubt he once coveted another's belongings. However, what he lacked was love and affection from his parents. They were so busy making money to give their children the good things of life that they had little time left to spend with them. As a result, feelings of envy and jealousy arose in him when he perceived I was not paying enough attention to him. I remember early in our marriage the times Fred would get upset if I went out with friends or spoke to groups of people. When I seemed to like the company of others more than being with him, he felt diminished and rejected because of his childhood issues.

As Christians, we know envy and jealousy are sins. Yet simply recognizing them as sin does little to prevent us from falling prey to these strong emotions again and again. If we truly hope to conquer emotions that cause us to belittle ourselves and act unkindly toward others, we first need to look at their source.

Roots That Run Deep

To overcome our feelings of envy and jealousy we need to understand their roots in our life. Trying to eradicate these negative attitudes without knowing why we experience them is like hunting without knowing what it is we're looking for.

Years into our marriage, Fred and I began tracing the source of our feelings of envy and jealousy. And we found, like many, our feelings stemmed from experiences in our childhood. In Fred's case, his jealousy of my time and friends stemmed from a sense of rejection from his parents, who sincerely thought they were doing what was right for him. Many of us, like Fred, grew up thinking we were unacceptable and not valued in our parents' eyes. If we grew up accepting that we were the dumb one, the plain one, the homely one, or the clumsy one, we as adults continue to believe the lies. "Perhaps my mother was right—maybe I'm not good-looking enough," or, "If I'm not attractive, maybe my husband will leave me for another woman."

One woman I know admitted to having an ongoing struggle with jealousy and of being suspicious that her husband was having an affair. When we traced the origins of her feelings, she realized that a lifetime of covering up for her philandering father caused her to mistrust men. "From the time I was a child my father would say to me, 'If you don't tell your mother that you saw me here, I'll give you a new toy.' "

Consequently, she was pampered excessively by her father and made the victim of jealous rages by her mother. Throughout her life, she has been engaged in a cycle of jealousy that began to play itself out in her marriage.

Jealousy and suspicion go hand in hand. If you're jealous of somebody, you're suspicious. You watch everything they do. Once you're caught in the jealousy/suspicion cycle, as with any other emotional problem, you need to stop and ask, "Where did I first get this idea?" Sit down and write a letter to God. You might say, "Dear Lord, when I think of myself, I don't feel that I am good-looking. Show me where this feeling comes from," or "Lord, I feel mistrustful of my husband. Help me understand where my suspicion arises from and whether or not it is legitimate."

The Lord does expect us to use our intelligence. One woman I talked with said her husband was a workaholic. He came home at three in the morning and left again at seven a.m. When I asked if she knew he was working that late every night, she answered that she had never checked because "a good Christian wife shouldn't be suspicious." Upon making a few phone calls, we found that he not only had another woman, but he had bought a house for her and was dividing his time between the two places. We need to use our minds and lay out our questions before the Lord. He will confirm suspicions or take away our fears. In the area of low self-esteem we need to go back and think, "Who was it that told me I was fat or that I couldn't sing?" Whenever we can tie together our feelings from the past—both positive and negative—with where we are today, it allows us to better understand why we view ourselves and our world as we do.

GIVE WHAT YOU'VE GOT

Each of us needs to focus on our uniqueness and give from the wealth of ourselves. You may not have grown up in an enormous home with statues and plush rugs, but you may be a warm, genuine person who can offer others simple hospitality and the warmth of your heart, which is far more important than any material object.

—*Luci*

Besides feeling rejected by our parents in our childhood, another root of our envy and jealousy is often what we craved as a child but never had. For me, it was a proper house to live in and nice clothes. Often when I'm speaking, I'll ask the audience to quickly write down the first three things that come to mind that they really needed as a child and didn't get—voids they still feel emotional about today. No one ever has trouble with this exercise, yet for many it is the first time they've ever consciously thought through the voids they still feel, and the first time they've realized how these lacks affect their attitudes and behavior today. Being Christians, most of us are geared toward giving rather than receiving, so to look at what we didn't receive feels somehow ungodly. Until we look at what we didn't get, though, we can't understand what it is we're really craving, and the envy and jealousy will continue to fester.

When Fred and I did this exercise, we realized that we married each other in part because the other represented a chance to fill those voids from our childhood. Without ever verbalizing our needs, we were looking for a particular response. Fred represented material comfort and security to me, and I supplied the affirmation he longed for to make up for his deep feelings of rejection. Once we discovered the hidden agenda each of us had brought to our relationship, we quickly realized why we had come up short on meeting each other's expectations.

Taking Out the Trash

Once we unearth the source of our envy or jealousy, we need to make it a matter of confession and prayer. The woman I described earlier with the philandering father was worried her husband would have an affair. Once she found where this fear came from she needed to pray, "Lord, I see now why I'm jealous of my husband. It's because I saw what my father did all those years to my mother. I realize jealousy is a problem in my life, and I ask you to take away this feeling and to help me forgive my father."

When we pray specifically for the emotional struggles we face, God can come in and clean up the dirt in our lives. But we have to put our needs before Him so He can know what areas we want purified. To draw an analogy, the garbage collector in my neighborhood faithfully arrives every Friday to haul away the trash. He comes when he says he will, he takes away the garbage, and he never brings it back. However, for this man to fulfill his function, I first must do my part: I have to bring the garbage to the curb. Likewise with God, He is always there, waiting to clean up the trash in my life. He will take it away and remember it no more, but I have to give it to Him first. He'll only take away what I put out.

So many times with emotional problems, we expect God to take away our trash, yet we refuse to walk it to the curb. We make no effort and hope the Lord will come in and empty our wastebaskets for us. 1 John 1:9 says, "If we confess our sins, he is faithful and just and will forgive us our sins and purify us [cleanse us] from all unrighteousness." When we agree with God and pray sincerely, the Lord will show us what the trash is so we can put it out and He can take it away. With His forgiveness, He even promises to clean out the can!

Sometimes Christians ask Fred and me, "Why should we look at childhood problems? Since we're new creatures in Christ, isn't it better to leave well enough alone?" Our research shows that seventy-five percent of the Christian women we deal with have suffered some kind of abuse as children, whether physical, sexual, or emotional. That means many of us are coming into adulthood with serious unresolved problems that often manifest themselves in jealousy, envy, or any number of compulsive and addictive behaviors.

Becoming a Christian doesn't automatically wipe out our past problems and make us perfect. If it did, we would have all our churches functioning in joyful harmony and all Christians would love one another.

When we commit our lives to the Lord Jesus, the Holy Spirit begins His creative and reconstructive powers in our lives. In order to achieve our spiritual potential, we have to be willing to be changed. We have to face the fact that we have weaknesses in our lives and bring them to the Lord. Oswald Chambers writes in *My Utmost for His Highest* (Barbour), "The moment you are willing that God should alter your disposition His re-creating forces will begin to work."

In my experience of working with thousands of women, I have found that admitting we have a problem that we can't handle in our own power is the first big step toward healing, followed by our willingness to change. Philippians 2:13 says, "God is always at work in you to make you willing and able to obey his good purpose" (TEV). When we are willing, He is able to bring miraculous change into our lives.

EVERYDAY DISHES WILL DO

I once had to host a dinner party for friends who were much more affluent than Steve and I. How would I ever measure up to their expectations of hospitality? I bought new kitchen curtains, I cleaned out drawers, terrified they might inspect my housekeeping. I obsessed over the fact that we don't have crystal or fine china. Finally, it occurred to me how self-centered I had become by comparing myself to others. I wasn't worried about making my guests feel comfortable but instead how I'd look. At that moment I resolved to host a simple, down-to-earth dinner party so that I would be free to enjoy our guests and focus on them rather than myself.

—Annie

One woman in my Bible study was in a depression over her sister's good fortunes when her own income was less. She asked me how to get over her envy. "I should be happy for her, but instead I'm furious," she admitted. We discussed their childhood and found she felt her sister got all the privileges and the best marks. "I've always been second fiddle and I'm sick of it," she said. I asked if she was willing to let God change her attitude, and she replied that she wasn't willing. I gave her Philippians 2:13 to memorize and asked if she was willing to be willing. She answered, "I'm not even willing to be willing to be willing!" The next week she returned and reported she was down to "two willings." She at least could laugh about it. The following week she was down to one willing and we prayed together over the verse. The bitterness and envy began to lift, and as her attitude changed, she started to help other women in the class who were still at "three willings." It's amazing what the Lord can do with each one of us once we become willing.

———————— ✑ ————————

Even though we are Christians, many of us remain plagued by feelings of envy and jealousy toward others. On our own, we can do little to conquer these sinful attitudes once and for all. But with Christ standing ready to forgive and cleanse us, we can experience the renewing of our hearts and minds and become transformed more closely into His image.

Make It Happen

1. Quickly call to mind the first three lacks you felt as a child. As you reflect on these unmet needs, do you see any connection between them and any continual struggles you experience as an adult with envy or jealousy? Write your insights in a prayer to God, asking Him to clean up whatever debris clutters your heart.

2. If you find yourself falling into the comparison trap, your self-esteem may need a lift. Call to mind the gifts you possess that are uniquely yours—patience, compassion, lightheartedness, hospitality. Focus on these and ask God to help you find ways to use your gifts for His glory.

3. You may covet your friend's material success and assume she has an easy life. However, the next time you're together take a few extra minutes to listen closely to her. Listen for those areas where she needs the compassion of a friend. Be open to others' weaknesses and stand ready to uphold them with your strength.

Admiration Gone Sour

Eileen Silva Kindig

Envy. Sooner or later it visits almost everyone. What makes it so difficult for us to rejoice in another's blessings? And more important, is it even possible to be content with our lot in life? Fortunately, the answer is yes, once you understand the mechanics of envy.

Although the words *envy* and *jealousy* are often used interchangeably, they're not the same. Envy has been aptly described as "admiration gone sour." It is feeling inadequate, depressed, and angry because you're "just" a housewife when your best friend has recently been named Businesswoman of the Year. Jealousy, on the other hand, is feeling angry, inadequate, and scared when someone threatens to take something from you. Neither emotion enhances our self-esteem, but envy is often the more demoralizing because of the guilt that inevitably accompanies it. Somehow it seems more Christian to want to hang on to something we value than it does to appear too greedy.

Psychologists say there are specific stages or degrees of envy. The first is covetousness, that painful demeaning wanting, which, if allowed to run rampant, can make mincemeat of our inner peace. Left unchecked, covetousness leads to resentment, which can turn into hatred. Unfortunately, envy often wears a clever mask.

My neighbor is an attractive, well-educated interior decorator with two adorable children and a successful husband. Her home is immaculate and color coordinated down to the dish towels. "She's so neurotic," I would say. So ardently did I believe my holier-than-thou attitude that I was speechless

161

when a friend casually commented, "Sounds like you feel you don't measure up." At first I hotly denied it. Finally, I had no choice but to admit it—envy was wading through my constant stream of criticism.

Psychologists say that when someone we know receives good fortune there's a "near miss" quality about it. We reason that such good fortune should have been bestowed on us. The sad result, of course, is that envy pushes away the very people who might enhance our lives the most and doesn't allow us to see their vulnerabilities.

It's difficult to live in a society where advertisements assail us with the message that we deserve it all. We begin to believe it. We use objects to fill inner voids instead of concentrating on what's really essential to our physical, mental, emotional, and spiritual well-being. The irony is that the more we try to bolster our egos with status goods and services, the more miserable and obsessed we become. Eliminating envy from our lives isn't easy, and sometimes it takes professional counsel to overcome it. But with effort, it can be done.

First, realize that no one has everything. Sometimes we are so overwhelmed by feelings of inadequacy that it seems as though everybody else "has it made." Remember my neighbor, the interior decorator? I was amazed to learn that her constant quest for perfection is really an effort to imitate the wife of her husband's boss, whom she desperately wants to be linked with socially. What I mistook for poise and confidence is actually envy traveling incognito.

Next, stop making comparisons. Concentrate on your own goals, values, and accomplishments. Share what you have. Even if you're convinced you have little or nothing, there's always someone who has less. Volunteer at a nursing home or food bank for a jolt of reality.

While envy seems to visit everybody sooner or later, it especially loves the idle. Too much time on our hands or not enough stimulus not only allows us to entertain envy, but also encourages us to share a roof with it. Involve yourself with family, friends, church, and community activities instead of roaming the shopping malls. Also, examine your values. What do you really want out of life? What things are most important? Given a choice, most of us would opt for "the good life," but at what price?

Make the most of who you are. You don't have to be the brightest, best looking, funniest, or most anything to be happy and fulfilled. Remember the parable about the talents in the Bible? It didn't matter how much each servant started out with—what mattered was what he did with it.

Don't let a day go by without thanking God for your blessings. Modern life has a way of demanding, pulling, and pushing until we get so enmeshed in what needs to be done that we forget what has been accomplished. That's why it's so important to set aside a time each day to take stock of the good things—the big ones like family, friends, and health, or a letter from a faraway friend.

—From *Today's Christian Woman* (September/October 1988)

13

Can I Ever Win the War Over Worry?

—Annie Chapman

GOD MUST HAVE KNOWN what a fundamental tendency worry is for us because Scripture is full of warnings against being anxious and advice on how to combat worry. Worry and anxiety cause everything from headaches and sick stomachs to phobias that actually paralyze people and keep them in their homes for years. For the Christian, worry has even greater consequences.

Worry is a potent emotion, as the disciple Luke noted, "The seed that fell among thorns stands for those who hear, but as they go on their way they are choked by life's worries, riches and pleasures, and they do not mature" (8:14). Worry actually chokes the Word of God from our hearts.

Besides creating a wall between us and God, worry, especially over inconsequential things, cripples us. In Greek, the word for worry is *merimnao*, which is a combination of two words—*merizo*, meaning to divide, and *nous*, which means mind. So, to worry is to divide the mind. James 1:6–8 says, "But when he asks, he must believe and not doubt, because he who doubts is like a wave of the sea, blown and tossed by the wind. That man should not think he will receive anything from the Lord;

he is a double-minded man, unstable in all he does." Literally, our minds are divided between trust and fear.

If you've been around a person who constantly worries, you know how unstable she is—both emotionally and spiritually. Emotionally, it doesn't take much to throw her into a state of anxiety, and spiritually, she's torn between focusing on her own fears and struggling with her unbelief in God's ability to provide.

God has promised over and over He won't desert us. He loves us more than we love ourselves. Yet, when we follow a path of worry, we make a liar of God. In essence, we're saying to Him, "I cannot trust your promises because you don't tell the truth. You will forsake me. You won't meet my needs." When we fail to put our trust in God, we're telling Him we could do a better job if we were in control. Since worry can be such a destructive emotion, it behooves us to get a handle on it.

Weapons Against Worry

Making the conscious choice not to worry is a key step in overcoming your tendency to worry. That said, it's not an easy choice. Many of us are so accustomed to carrying the burden of responsibility for our families' happiness, safety, and well-being that it becomes difficult to transfer the ultimate responsibility for these things to the one who really is in control—God.

If you catch yourself falling into the worry trap, it helps to dwell on 2 Corinthians 10:5: "We demolish arguments and every pretension that sets itself up against the knowledge of God, and we take captive every thought to make it obedient to Christ." This is more than just a mental exercise in positive thinking. When troubling thoughts start to invade our minds, we need to choose to let them go. Out of obedience and reverence to Christ, we must simply refuse to worry.

WORRIED SICK

Harold traveled a lot when our children were young. During one trip, for some reason, I became completely irrational with anxiety and fear. All I could think was, What will happen if he's killed and I have these four young children to raise by myself? I obsessed about this fear to the point of illness. Finally, a Christian friend came over to pray for me. She said, "Satan is using this to destroy you and to make you absolutely useless in the kingdom of God. This spirit of fear needs to be broken in you." She prayed with me, and as I focused on the Lord and His power to free me, I could feel the fear drain out of me. I have never been immobilized by that fear again.

—Luci

I still wrestle with this. Not long ago, Steve took the children on a two-day fishing trip in the middle of the Gulf of Mexico. I didn't go because I can't stand the smell of fish and, besides, I felt that tying the boat up each night to an oil rig in the middle of the Gulf wasn't very safe. At the same time, I knew that raising a stink about the trip would only deprive them of a memorable experience. It took all of the self-control I could muster to bite my tongue and prevent them from going. The first night they were gone, I laid in bed and stared at the ceiling. I had visions of them shipwrecked and marooned on some deserted island. In the end, everything turned out fine, but it was hard for me not to let my fears about the trip keep them from going in the first place, and then to not let worry overcome me while they were gone. Worry and trust cannot coexist. One will win over the other.

———— ✺ ————

One of the surest ways to combat worry is to seek God's will for our lives. Many times we don't trust God in every situation because we haven't consulted Him about the details of our lives. For instance, many mothers who work outside the home worry obsessively about their children during the day. Granted, it's natural to have fleeting worries about our children when they're out of our sight. However, the woman who lives in constant anxiety over her child's well-being may actually be uncomfortable with her choice to work.

We won't experience the peace that comes with following God's will unless we've sought His will in the first place. If we seek God's will, and we're confident that we're acting according to His will, it's much easier to let go of worry and trust He will keep His promises.

When Nathan went on a two-week missions trip to Russia at age fourteen, I had peace because I was confident he was in God's will. Likewise, when Nathan and Heidi spent two weeks in Venezuela this past summer, I refused to worry because I was confident they were in God's will.

Another way to replace worry with peace is to fill our minds with the truth. When we say "no" to worry, God blesses us with a peace that is not our own. But that peace comes only when we take action—when we renew our minds each day. We are taught in Proverbs 3:5–6, "Trust in the Lord with all your heart and lean not on your own understanding; in all your ways acknowledge him, and he will make your paths straight." Learning to cast away the lies that we've been taught and replacing them with the truth of Scripture takes deliberate work. It's tough to change our thought patterns, but with God's help we can do it.

We are to fill our minds with whatever is true, noble, right, pure, lovely, admirable—anything that is excellent and praiseworthy (Philippians 4:8). That means we should meditate on Scripture. Verses that speak of God's love for us, such as Psalm 34:4 and Psalm 139:17–18, 23–24, are good ones to commit to memory, so you will be prepared to fight off the temptation to worry. In the same regard, filling our minds with the bizarre perversions of talk shows and the gossip-mill magazines gives fuel to worry and concern. This flesh food feeds our anxieties.

In his book *How to Win Over Worry* (Harvest House), Scott Haggai says, "Worry is a weakness of the flesh. You cannot conquer a weakness of the flesh in the energy of the flesh. It must be done in the power of God. Prayer gives you access to that power." Only God can overcome the weakness of the flesh.

I worry every time I enter an airport that we will lose our luggage, miss our plane, or experience some mishap. Steve and the kids know I struggle with worry when we travel, so I've tried to use my weakness in this area to teach the kids how to let go of worry and use prayer to combat it.

When something goes wrong, I've said, "Look, my natural inclination is to worry about this, but I want you to pray with me because I am choosing not to worry about this. Will you help me?"

Recently, we lost our luggage, and I knew the kids were looking at me, wondering if I was going to fly off the handle. Thankfully, I'm making progress. I've learned to contain myself better when things go wrong. Occasionally, I'll ask Steve and the kids, "Do you think I'm getting better?" I want their input, and I need to be encouraged. I also want them to know that life is a process and you're never too old to work at overcoming a weakness.

I've found that when I focus on the needs and the problems of others, I seem to worry less about myself. Perhaps part of our tendency to worry stems from thinking too much about ourselves. On the other hand, when we're focused on giving to others, we're much more apt to praise God and recognize His hand in the world.

I once heard a story about a man who was robbed. Instead of fretting about the terrible thing that had happened to him, he had four praises: This was the first time he had been robbed; the thieves had taken his money instead of his life; he didn't have much money for them to take; and he was the one being robbed instead of the one robbing.

For every circumstance that appears as a misfortune on the surface, there is a flip side—one that induces praise and thanksgiving. When it comes to combating the habit of worry, we need to be dwelling on that new perspective.

Our lifestyle can induce a spirit of anxiety as much as our mental attitude. Along with working on reprogramming our thoughts, regular exercise can help eliminate the negative physical side effects of anxiety such as high blood pressure, heart trouble, stomach disorders, migraine headaches, and a host of other medical problems. Worry turns to sin when we allow it to destroy the temple of the Spirit living inside us.

I've also found that planning ahead and being prepared goes a long way toward keeping me out of the panic mode. For instance, when we entertain, I always try to do as much of the work ahead of time as possible so I can rest before our guests arrive. If I'm rested, I can enjoy our company instead of feeling uptight during their visit. I had a birthday party for Steve recently, and it fell on the same day we were recording an album, the manuscript for my book was due, and we had just returned from a trip. Knowing we would be away all weekend and to save myself from feeling frenzied, I set the table for the party the Thursday before. I also prepared as much of the food as I could ahead of time. In the end, I was able to enjoy our party as much as our guests did.

LET GOD BE GOD

By nature women are concerned over their children and want the best for each of them, but when concern moves into worry it can easily become an obsession. We need to do the best we can and leave the result to God. We need to concentrate on our relationship with the Lord and not worry about what others will think. Author Oswald Chambers once wrote, "Worrying means that we do not think that God can look after the practical details of our lives, and it is never anything else that worries us."

—Florence

Looking to the Future With a Smile

The virtuous woman in Proverbs 31 is described as a woman who "looks at the future and smiles." I am faced with a mother who has cancer and a dad whose heart disease has ravaged his body, leaving him with 20% use of his heart. I'm struggling to raise two teenagers in a society bereft of any moral backbone, and soon my son will be old enough to be drafted. When I look to the future, all I feel is anxiety.

"How does the Proverbs 31 woman smile about the future?" I questioned aloud one day to a friend. Gently, my friend said, "She faces the future with a smile because she trusts in the Lord."

My friend was right. The only way you can deal with worry and fear is to put your trust in the God who holds tomorrow. Again, worry and fear cannot coexist with trust. It's like forgiveness, it's a divine act. Anything that requires more strength than we humanly possess is difficult because we're forced to entrust ourselves to God. When we choose not to worry, we're giving God the right to take care of us. We're telling Him that no matter what might happen to us, we believe He is all-knowing and all-powerful, and His way is best.

Second Timothy 1:7 says, "For God did not give us a spirit of timidity, but a spirit of power, of love and of self-discipline." God is powerful enough to be in control, so we don't have to live our lives wringing our hands.

Make It Happen

1. Write down all the things that cause you to feel anxious. As you look over the list, imagine the worst thing that could happen in each circumstance. Next, list any positive things that could come from these situations. Commit your list of fears to God, and ask Him to show you the good in difficult circumstances.

2. Search the Scriptures for verses that build your faith and help you let go of worry. Romans 8:28 or Isaiah 40:28–31 are good ones to start with. Write the verses on an index card and keep them with you at all times. Whenever you feel yourself starting to worry, pull out the cards and regroup.

3. If you have sincerely turned your worries over to God, but your worst fears have still come true, take some time to consider ways in which God has been present, even though circumstances may not be what you had hoped for. Praise God for the goodness you have experienced and continue to look for opportunities to give Him thanks.

EPILOGUE

FEARFULLY AND WONDERFULLY MADE

UNDERSTANDING HOW AND WHY we respond emotionally to the different situations and circumstances each of us faces in our daily life can be a complex process. As you begin to unravel the mystery of your own emotional makeup, you will discover key principles Annie, Luci, and Florence have given. First, emotions, in and of themselves, are not wrong or bad. God equipped us with the ability to feel and experience a range of emotions as a means of drawing us closer to Him. The more we become attuned to God's purpose in allowing us to feel specific emotions, and the more we allow Him to control our hearts and minds, the more our emotions will guide us to a Christlike life.

Second, bringing our emotions under submission to God and using them for His glory is often easier said than done. A theme repeated frequently in the pages of this book is, when it comes to handling our emotions, we have a choice. God desires for us to use our emotions in constructive ways. However, when we make the wrong choice and allow our emotions to lead us to sin, we can be thankful that Christ stands ready to forgive. The barrier that our unchecked emotions can cause between us and God does not have to remain. All three women continually remind us to seek the face of God, even when our emotions cause us to sin, so that our emotions can serve as a blessing rather than a curse. By humbly presenting our failures to the Lord, He will renew us and give us strength to respond appropriately with our emotions in the future.

Finally, each of the contributors sounded a clarion call: know thyself. By analyzing the results of the personality quiz, delving into the past, and journaling daily feelings and experiences, each of us can gain insight into why we respond as we do to certain people, events, and circumstances.

Jesus felt everything we feel. He knows the struggles each of us face as we try to keep our emotions under submission to Him. With the insights of Annie, Florence, and Luci, coupled with the Word of God, we go well-armed to fight against the pitfalls of emotions and to celebrate the gift of being "fearfully and wonderfully made."

Today's Christian Woman is a positive, practical magazine designed for contemporary Christian women of all ages, single or married, who seek to live out biblical values in their homes, workplaces, and communities. With honesty and warmth, *Today's Christian Woman* provides depth, balance, and perspective to the issues that confront women today.

If you would like a subscription to *Today's Christian Woman* send your name and address to:

TODAY'S CHRISTIAN WOMAN
P.O. Box 11618
Des Moines, IA 50340

Subscription rates:
    one year (6 issues) $14.95
    two years (12 issues) $23.60